Surrey & Sussex

Occupations

A Genealogical Guide

Stuart A. Raymond

Surrey & Sussex: The Genealogists Library Guide 5

Published by the
Federation of Family History Societies (Publications) Ltd.
Units 15-16, Chesham Industrial Centre
Oram Street, Bury
Lancashire, BL9 6EN, UK

Copies also available from:
S.A. & M.J. Raymond
P.O.Box 35, Exeter, Devon EX1 3YZ, U.K.
Email: stuart@samjraymond.softnet.co.uk
Website: http://www.soft.net.uk/samjraymond/igb.htm

First published 2001

ISBN: 1 86006 145 1 (FFHS (Publications) Ltd.)
ISBN: 1 899668 21 7 (S.A. & M.J. Raymond)

ISSN: 1033-2065

Printed and bound by The Alden Group, Oxford and Northampton.

Contents

Front cover: Clapham Junction

Introduction

A considerable amount of occupational information on Surrey and Sussex men and women is available in print. Biographical dictionaries, record publications, regimental histories, guides to sources, *etc.*, all help us to identify people in the past, and may provide essential clues in tracing our family trees. The purpose of this bibliography is to draw these publications to the attention of the genealogist. Unpublished works are not listed here. Arrangement is alphabetical by occupation. The term 'occupation' is interpreted liberally, including, for example, club members, freemasons, *etc.* With a few exceptions, works listed in my *Occupational sources for genealogists* are excluded; this volume should also be consulted. I have physically examined every item cited, except where I have noted 'not seen'.

Many books are available which simply describe or analyse a particular occupation; in general, such works are not listed here, since they are not of direct genealogical interest. Many histories of particular businesses are also available, but are mostly not listed here.

The great majority of the works that I have listed are readily available. Some titles you may be able to purchase; all can be found in libraries throughout the English-speaking world. You can check the holdings of many libraries via their catalogues on the internet; alternatively, if your local library does not hold a particular book, the librarian should be able to tell you where to find it — and, as a last resort, may be able to borrow it for you via the inter-library loan network, irrespective of whether you live in London or San Francisco. The libraries of family history societies are also worth checking — even if they are far distant from Southern England: for example, the Genealogical Society of Victoria, in Melbourne, has a good collection of books on English genealogy. Some family history societies offer a postal borrowing service; others may be willing to check a particular book for you. It is also worth joining one of the genealogical newsgroups or mailing lists on the internet; other members may hold the books you need, and be willing to check them for you.

This is the 5th volume of *Surrey and Sussex: the genealogists library guide*, which aims to provide a comprehensive listing of every published work likely

4

to be of interest to researchers tracing ancestors in these two counties. The other volumes may contain material which is pertinent to this volume, but in general the information they contain is not repeated here.

In compiling this bibliography, I have visited many libraries. Extensive use has been made of the resources of Exeter University Library, Surrey History Centre, Guildhall Library, the Society of Genealogists, and Exeter Public Library. I have visited the local studies departments of public libraries in Brighton, Brixton, Chichester, Croydon, Eastbourne, Hastings, Richmond, Southwark, and Worthing, and also the West Sussex Record Office. A variety of other libraries have also been visited. My thanks go to the librarians of all these institutions for their assistance. The manuscript was typed by Cynthia Hanson; Martin Hayes and Cliff Webb kindly checked the manuscript for obvious errors and omissions, and the book has been seen through the press by Bob Boyd. My thanks go to all these people, and also to the officers of the Federation of Family History Societies, without whose support this series could not be published. Any errors that remain — and I am sure there will be some — are my sole responsibility, and I would be grateful if they could be brought to my attention. If you come across any work that I have omitted which you think ought to be included, please let me know.

Stuart A. Raymond

Bibliographic Presentation

Authors' names are in SMALL CAPITALS. Book and journal titles are in *italics.* Articles appearing in journals, and essays, *etc.,* forming only parts of books, are in inverted commas. Volume numbers are shown in **bold,** and the individual numbers of journals may be shown in parentheses. In the case of articles, further figures indicate page numbers. Book titles are normally followed by the place of publication (except where this is London, which is omitted), the name of the publisher, and the date of publication.

Abbreviations

B.R.L.H.S.N.	*Bognor Regis Local History Society newsletter*
D.P.H.S.M.	*Danehill Parish Historical Society magazine*
E.L.H.	*Eastbourne Local Historian*
E.L.H.S.N.	*Eastbourne Local History Society newsletter*
E.Sy.F.H.S.J.	*East Surrey Family History Society journal*
F.M.S.Q.N.	*Farnham Museum Society quarterly newsletter*
F.H.S.	Family History Society
F.R.	*Family Roots*
H. & R.F.H.S.J.	*Hastings & Rother Family History Society [journal]*
L.H.R.	*Local history records for Caterham and Warlingham, Coulsdon and Purley [Bourne Society local history records]*
N.S.	New Series
P.L.D.L.H.S.	*Proceedings of the Leatherhead & District Local History Society*
R. & B.	*Root and branch [West Surrey F.H.S. journal]*
Sx.A.C	*Sussex archaeological collections*
Sx.A.S.N.	*Sussex Archaeological Society newsletter*
Sx.F.H.	*Sussex family historian*
Sx.G.L.H.	*Sussex genealogist and local historian*
Sx.N.Q.	*Sussex notes and queries*
Sx.R.S.	Sussex Record Society
Sy.A.C	*Surrey archaeological collections*
Sy.R.S.	Surrey Record Society
W.Sx.H.	*West Sussex history*

Libraries and Record Offices

There are numerous libraries with substantial book collections relating to Surrey and Sussex. For the present (post-1974) county of Surrey, the major library is the Surrey History Centre; however, boundary changes mean that there are also 6 London metropolitan boroughs in historic Surrey, all of which have specialist local history collections. Most public libraries also have some local history materials.

For Sussex, most of the major town libraries have substantial local history collections, as do the Record Offices of East and West Sussex. The libraries at Worthing and Brighton probably have the most substantial collections.

Collections relating to Surrey and Sussex may also be found in many other public and university libraries throughout the country (and, indeed, the world), as well as at specialist institutions such as the Society of Genealogists and the British Library. The local family history societies also have small libraries.

The list which follows concentrates on those libraries within the historic counties, and is very selective.

SURREY

Surrey History Centre,
130, Goldsworth Road,
Woking,
Surrey, GU21 1ND

Croydon
Croydon Library & Archives Service,
Katharine Street,
Croydon,
Surrey, CR9 1ET

Kingston on Thames
Local History Centre,
Heritage Centre,
Wheatfield Way,
Kingston on Thames,
Surrey, KT1 2PS

Lambeth
Minet Library,
52, Knatchbull Road,
Brixton,
London, SE5 9QY

Merton
Merton Local Studies Centre,
Merton Civic Centre,
London Road,
Morden,
Surrey, SM4 5DX

Richmond
Richmond Local Studies Library,
Central Reference Library,
Old Town Hall,
Whittaker Avenue,
Richmond,
Surrey, TW9 1TP

Southwark
Southwark Local Studies
  Library,
211, Borough High Street,
Southwark,
London,
SE1 1JA

Sutton
Sutton Archives,
Central Library,
St.Nicholas Way,
Sutton,
Surrey,
SM1 1EA

Wandsworth
Wandsworth Local History
  Collection,
Battersea Library,
265, Lavender Hill
London, SW11 1JB

SUSSEX

East Sussex Record Office,
The Maltings,
Castle Precincts,
Lewes,
Sussex, BN7 1YT

West Sussex Record Office,
County Hall,
Chichester,
PO19 1RN

Brighton
Brighton Local Studies Library,
Church Street,
Brighton,
Sussex, BN1 1UD

Chichester
Local Studies Collection,
West Sussex County Library,
Tower Street,
Chichester,
Sussex, PO19 1QJ

Eastbourne
Local Studies Collection,
Eastbourne Library,
Grove Road,
Eastbourne,
Sussex, BN21 4LT

Hastings
Local Studies Collection,
Hastings Library,
Brassey Institute,
13, Claremont,
Hastings, TN34 1HE

Lewes
Sussex Room,
Lewes Library,
Albion Street,
Lewes,
Sussex, BN7 2ND

Worthing
Local Studies Library
Worthing Library,
Richmond Road,
Worthing,
Sussex, BN11 1HD

Surrey and Sussex Occupations

Advertisers
MASLEN, KATE. 'Small ads as a source for family history', *R. & B.* **10**(3), 1983, 97-9. Lists names of Surrey advertisers in *The English mechanic and mirror of science* for 1869-70.

Agricultural Labourers
See Farmers

Apothecaries
WHITTET, T. DOUGLAS. 'Sussex apothecaries' tokens and their issuers', *W.Sx.H.* **37**, 1987, 1-7.

Apprentices
RICE, R. GARRAWAY, ed. *Sussex apprentices and masters 1710 to 1752.* Sx.R.S. **28**. 1924.
JENKINSON, HILARY, ed. *Surrey apprenticeships from the registers in the Public Record Office 1711-1731.* Sy.R.S. **10**. 1921. Also issued as no. **30** of the Society's publications.
WEBB, CLIFF, ed. *An index to Surrey apprenticeships, volume II, 1731-1749 (being a continuation of Surrey Record Society volume X, 1929).* West Surrey F.H.S., record publications **6**, 1985.
The two Surrey works cited above are reprinted in:
Surrey apprenticeships, 1711-1749, being a reprint on three microfiche of Surrey apprenticeships, 1711-1731, ed Hilary Jenkinson (Surrey Record Society 10 1929), and Surrey apprenticeships II, 1731-1749, ed Cliff Webb (West Surrey Family History Society RS6, 1985). 3 fiche in folder. Microfiche series **12**. West Surrey F.H.S., 1996.
WEBB, CLIFF. *Surrey apprentices III, being an index of apprenticeships of Surrey interest in some London livery company records, 1563-1928.* West Surrey Family History Society record series **33**. 2000.

Ashburnham
'Ashburnham parish apprentices 1585-1751', *Sx.G.L.H.* **5**(2), 1983, 75. List of 36 apprentices.

Battersea
O'SULLIVAN, MAUREEN. *Battersea, Surrey. Index to apprenticeship records, 1602-1902.* East Surrey F.H.S. record publication **24**. 1988.

Croydon
SHAW, HERBERT, & O'SULLIVAN, MAUREEN. *Croydon, Surrey. Indexes to apprenticeship registers, 1802-1843; census, 1811.* 1 fiche. East Surrey F.H.S. record publication **3**. 1987.

Farnham
HEWINS, MAURICE. 'Some poor boys apprenticed by Farnham parish', *R & B* 3(3), 1977, 101-2. 1804-11.

Guildford Union
'From the Parliamentary Commission report on the Employment of women and children in agriculture 1842: apprentices bound in 30 parishes of Guildford Union within last eight years', *R. & B.* **18**(2), 1991, 51. List of apprentices and their masters.

Kingston on Thames
DALY, ANNE, ed. *Kingston upon Thames register of apprentices, 1563-1713.* Sy.R.S. **28**. 1974.

Lambeth
GALLAGHER, SHEILA. 'Lambeth pauper apprenticeships, 1782-1856', *E.Sy.F.H.S.J.* **14**(1), 1991, 27-9. General discussion.

Lewes
THOMAS, EMLYN G. 'Lewes pauper apprentices', *Sx.G.L.H.* **1**(4), 1980, 126-33. Includes catalogue of 60 apprentices.

Mayfield

'Mayfield apprentices 1612-1812', *Sx.F.H.* 3(6), 1978, 175-8; 3(7), 1978, 206-10. Calendar of 117 apprenticeship bonds and indentures.

Mortlake

O'SULLIVAN, MAUREEN. *Mortlake, Surrey. Indexes to: apprenticeship records 1614-1915 (S.R.O. ref. 2414/6); poor law records 1631-1834 (S.R.O. ref. 2412/6); militia records 1801-1809 (S.R.O. ref. 2414/8/24-26).* 2 fiche. East Surrey F.H.S. record publication **11**. 1987.

Reigate

O'SULLIVAN, MAUREEN. *Reigate, Surrey. Indexes to: apprenticeship records, 1672-1796 (S.R.O. ref P49/9); poor law records 1669-1794 (S.R.O. ref P49/4).* 2 fiche. East Surrey F.H.S. record publication **9**. 1987.

Steyning

See Worth

Walton

EEDLE, MARIE DE G. *Some indications from the apprenticeship records for N.W. Surrey, 1711-1731.* Walton & Weybridge Local History Society monograph **9**. 1970. Duplicated typescript. Lists Walton and Weybridge apprentices and their masters.

Weybridge

See Walton

Wimbledon

O'SULLIVAN, MAUREEN. *Wimbledon, Surrey. Indexes to: apprenticeship indentures 1690-1895 (S.R.O. ref: P5/5/962-969, P5/14/1-26 & P5/17/9-30); poor law records 1698-1842 (S.R.O. ref P5/5, P5/14 & P5/17)* 2 fiche. East Surrey F.H.S. record publication **10**. 1987.

Worth

THOMAS, EMLYN. 'Pauper apprenticeship in West Sussex', *West Sussex Archives Society newsletter* **14**, 1979, 5-7. At Worth and Steyning; brief discussion, 17-19th c.
'Worth parish apprentices 1614-1741', *Sx.G.L.H.* 3(1), 1981, 30-33. Includes list.

Archaeologists

PHILLIPS, PAULINE. 'The participation of women in the journal *Sussex archaeological collections,* 1900-1950', *Sx.A.C.* **136**, 1998, 133-47.

Architects

see Botanists

Artists

BEASLEY, MAUREEN. *Five centuries of artists in Sutton: a biographical dictionary of artists associated with Sutton, London.* Sutton: Sutton Libraries & Arts Services, 1989.
See also Authors

Athletes

CALLIS, R. DASSETT. *The first hundred years of Ranelagh Harriers, founded 1881.* Ranelagh Harriers, 1980. Includes names of many cross country runners.

Authors

HANDLEY-TAYLOR, GEOFFREY. *Sussex authors today: being a checklist of authors born in Sussex, together with brief particulars of authors born elsewhere who are currently working or residing in Sussex ... an assemblage of more than 620 authors together with their addresses and (where applicable) their pseudonyms.* Eddison Press, 1973.
O'NEILL, MARTIN. *West Sussex literary, musical & artistic links.* New ed. Chichester: West Sussex County Council, 1996.

Bankers

HILL, ALAN F. 'A Lewes banking house: an outline of the development of the private bankers, Messrs. Whitfield, Molineux and Co., who traded as the Lewes Old Bank from 1789-1896', *Sussex industrial history* **24**, 1994, 25-9. Includes names of bankers.
PLUCK, JOHN. 'Friend or foe: a brief account of banking in Bognor and district', *B.R.L.H.S.N.* **21**, 1989, 24-7. 19-20th c.

Bankrupts

KNOWLES, FRANK. 'Sussex bankrupts extracted from the *Gentlemans magazine, Sx.F.H.* **5**(8), 1983, 261; **6**(1), 1984, 34-5; **6** (6), 1985, 230. 1731-89.

Bedmakers

MYER, EWART. *Myers first century, 1876-1976: the story of Myers comfortable beds.* Horatio Myer & Co., 1976. Of Vauxhall; includes pedigree of Myer family, and many names of bed-makers.

Bellfounders

SMALE, F.C. 'Bell-founders in Sussex', *Sussex county magazine* **9**, 1935, 16-18. 16-18th c.

Blacksmiths

NEALE, KENNETH. 'Village blacksmiths and their home, West Chiltington, Sussex', *Sussex history* **2**(10), 1985, 34-43. Descent of the smithy.

Bleachers

See Whitsters

Booksellers

PIPER, A. CECIL. 'The booksellers and printers of Richmond, Surrey', *The library* 4th series, **13**, 1933, 201-7. Includes list, 18-20th c.

Botanists

DESMOND, RAY. *Kew: the history of the Royal Botanic Gardens.* Harvill Press, 1995. Includes 'brief biographies' of persons associated with Kew — royalty, benefactors, directors, gardeners, plant collectors, flower painters, architects and garden designers, *etc.*

Brewers

Brighton

HOLTHAM, PETER. 'Seven Brighton brewers', *Sussex industrial history* **22**, 1922, 9-13.

East Grinstead

LEPPARD, M.J. 'Brewing in East Grinstead', *Bulletin of the East Grinstead Society* **31**, 1981, 7-8. 16-19th c.

Guildford

STURLEY, MARK. *The breweries and public houses of Guildford, with some notes on the temperance movement.* 2 vols. Guildford: Charles W. Traylen, 1990-95. Extensive; many names of brewers, innkeepers etc.

Brickmakers

BESWICK, M. *Brickmaking in Sussex: a history and gazetteer.* Heathfield: M. Beswick, 1993.

BESWICK, MOLLY. 'Brickmaking at Ridgewood', *Hindsight: the journal of the Uckfield & District Preservation Society* **3**, 1997, 4-10. Ware family, 18-20th c.

BESWICK, MOLLIE. & HODSOLL, VERA. 'Brickmaking and brickmakers in the Eastbourne area', *E.L.H.S.N.* **50**, 1983, 4-7.

LEPPARD, M.J. 'Brickmaking in East Grinstead', *Bulletin of the East Grinstead Society* **27**, 1979, 9-10. See also **44**, 1988, 3; **54**, 1994, 9-10; **55**, 1994, 6; **61**, 1997, 13.

Bridge Builders

JOHNSTON, G.D. 'Inscriptions on Sussex bridges', *Sx.N.Q.* **17**, 1968-71, 209-33. Identifying bridge builders, *etc.*

Building tradesmen, *etc.*

JENKINSON, HILARY. 'Chertsey Abbey after the dissolution', *Sy.A.C.* **28**, 1915, 29-40. Includes extracts from accounts, with a list of men employed in building works.

RAWLINGS, D.S. 'The men who built the church', *D.P.H.S.M.* **4**(11), 1993, 27-32. List of masons, labourers, *etc.* from the 1891 census (when the church was being built) for Danehill.

STEVENS, ROY. 'Building workmen at Arundel Castle on 13th March 1856'. *Sx.F.H.* **6**(5), 1985, 174-5.

Calico Printers

See Whitsters

Carriers

LUCAS, P.G. 'Local carriers in the 19th century', *D.P.H.S.M.* **4**(4), 1991, 27-34. At Danehill.

MEPHAM, TED. 'Hastings carriers' *H. & R.F.H.S.* **1**(2), 1996, 31-2. Includes list from *Pike's directory, 1922.*

Charcoalburners

ARMSTRONG, LYN. *Woodcolliers and charcoal burning.* Horsham: Coach Publishing House; Singleton: Weald & Downland Open Air Museum, 1978.

Clock and Watch Makers

LEPPARD, M.J. 'Watch and clockmakers in East Grinstead', *Bulletin of the East Grinstead Society* **10**, 1972, 9. See also 11, 1973, 14; **13**, 1973, 4; **19**, 1976, 14; **30**, 1981, 7; **31**, 1981, 4; **33**, 1982, 4.

LEPPARD, MICHAEL. 'East Grinstead clockmakers', *Sx.G.L.H.* **3**(1), 1981, 23-4. Includes list, 1693-1885.

TYLER, E.J. *The clockmakers of Sussex.* Watch & Clock Book Society, [198-?] Biographical dictionary.

TYLER, E.J. 'Sussex clockmakers', *Sx.G.L.H.* **2**(4), 1981, 157-63.

Cloth Workers

LEPPARD, M.J. 'Cloth working in East Grinstead', *Bulletin of the East Grinstead Society* **22**, 1977, 9-10. 16-19th c.

Club Members

GRANTHAM, W., & FEARON, J.F. *Sussex Club: list of past and present members, 1799-1949.* [ ]: the Club, 1949.

Coastguards

MILTON, ROSEMARY. 'Coastguard information from local records' *Family tree magazine* **8**(1), 1991, 30. Based on Sussex records.

MILTON, F.R. *Index to parish register entries concerning coast guards and their associates in the Eastbourne area, c.1813-c.1841.* Coastguard series **2**. [Eastbourne]: Family Roots F.H.S. (Eastbourne & District), 1989.

MILTON, F.R. *Index to coast guards in the district of Eastbourne, taken from the censuses 1831-1891.* [Eastbourne]: Family Roots F.H.S. (Eastbourne & District), 1994. Supplement to Coastguard series, part 1.

MILTON, F.R. *Index to coast guards working on a 16 mile stretch of Sussex coast round Eastbourne, taken from the census for Eastbourne & district, 1841, 51, 61, 71 and 81.* Coastguard series **1**. Eastbourne: Family Roots F.H.S. (Eastbourne & District), [198-?].

'Coastguardsmen's families in S.E.Dorset with Sussex birthplaces', *Sx.F.H.* **4**(1), 1979, 7-8. Extracts from the 1851 census.

Cricketers

ALEXANDER, M.B. *A history of the Honor Oak Cricket & Lawn Tennis Club, 1866-1965.* [The Club], 1965. Many names of players.

ALVERSTONE, LORD. *Surrey cricket: its history and associations.* Longmans, Green and Co., 1904. Includes various lists of cricketers.

BAILEY, PHILIP, & THORN, PHILIP. *Sussex cricketers 1815-1990.* Nottingham: Association of Cricket Statisticians, 1990. List, with brief notes.

CROIX, W.D.ST. 'On the archaeology of Sussex cricket', *Sx.A.C.* **28**, 1878, 59-82. Includes pedigree of Lillywhite, 18-19th c.

HILL, A. *The family fortune: a saga of Sussex cricket.* Shoreham by Sea: Scan Books, 1978. Many names of cricketers.

HOLMES, R.S. *Surrey cricket and cricketers 1773 to 1895.* Cricket, 1896. Many names listed.

LEMMON, DAVID. *The official history of Surrey County Cricket Club.* Christopher Helm, 1989. Includes brief 'biographical details of Surrey players'.

MCCANN, TIMOTHY J. 'The 4th Duke of Richmond and the great cricket match at Goodwood in 1814', *W.Sx.H.* **54**, 1994, 15-17. Includes list of cricketers.

MCCANN, TIMOTHY J., & WILKINSON, PETER M. 'The cricket match at Boxgrove in 1622', *Sx.A.C.* **110**, 1972, 118-22. Names cricketers cited to appear before the Consistory Court at Chichester for playing cricket in the churchyard.

SQUIRE, H.F., & SQUIRE, A.P. *Henfield cricket and its Sussex cradle.* Hove: Combridges, 1949. Includes list of 'members who have played for Henfield'.

WAKLEY, B.J. *The history of the Wimbledon Cricket Club, 1854-1953.* Bournemouth: Sydenhams, 1954. Many names of cricketers.

Criminals and Convicts

WELLS, ROGER. 'Popular protest and social crime: the evidence of criminal gangs in rural southern England, 1790-1860', *Southern history* **13**, 1991, 32-81. Predominantly in Sussex, Surrey and Kent; many names.

TAMBLIN, STUART. *Criminal register indexes 1805-1816. Volume twenty: Surrey.* 5 fiche. Northampton: Stuart Tamblin, 1999.

TAMBLIN, STUART. *Criminal register indexes 1805-1816. Volume twenty-two: Sussex.* 2 fiche. Northampton: Stuart Tamblin, 1999.

O'SULLIVAN, MAUREEN. 'Impressed men at Southwark Gaol, 1756', *E.Sy.F.H.S.J.* 1(1), 1988, 39. List.

WALCOT, MICHAEL. 'Prisoners on the Stirling Castle', *R. & B.* 2(1), 1975, 19-20. Prison hulk; names from Berkshire, Surrey *etc.*

GIBSON, DAVID. 'The treadmill', *R. & B.* 22(1), 1995, 25-6. Includes list of persons sentenced to the treadmill at Guildford, 1823.

Hastings gaol records: prisoners committed 1832-1841. Eastbourne: PBN Publications, 1990.

Hastings gaol records: keepers' commitment book 1842-1849. Eastbourne: PBN Publications, 1992.

Hastings gaol records: keepers' commitment book 1850-1853; allowance of food to prisoners, 1850-1852. Eastbourne: PBN Publications, 1993.

See also Emigrants

Creditors

CLUSE, JANE LE. 'The bankruptcy of R. Wood, of Shipley, grocer', *W.Sx.H.* 54, 1994, 23-4. Includes list of creditors, 1893, with biographical notes.

Customs & Excisemen

HATTER, L.A.B. 'List of collectors (H.M. Customs & Excise), Rye', *Sx.F.H.* 10(8), 1993, 326. For 1670-1950.

MILTON, F.R. *The fight against smuggling around Eastbourne and Newhaven.* Eastbourne: Family Roots F.H.S. (Eastbourne & District), 1991. Many names of customs and excise men.

PINK, JOHN. *The Excise officers and their duties in an English market town: Kingston upon Thames, 1643-1973.* New ed. Surbiton: JRP, 1995.

Domestics

See Labourers *and* Servants

East India Men

VIBART, H.M. *Addiscombe: its heroes and men of note.* A. Constable & Co., 1894. The school of the East India Company. Includes 'a brief record of the services of distinguished officers', 'a list of all the cadets who passed through Addiscombe', *etc.*

Emigrants

MCCANN, A.M. ed. *Emigrants and transportees from West Sussex, 1675-1889.* 2nd ed. West Sussex Record Office lists and indexes 10. Chichester: West Sussex County Council, 1984.

COOPER, W. DURRANT. 'Extracts from the passage-book of the port of Rye, 1635-6', *Sx.A.C.* 18, 1866, 170-9. Lists passengers travelling to the continent.

GRANT, R.C. 'Admissions registers to St. Joseph's Roman Catholic School, 1891-1938', *Sx.F.H.* 10(8), 1993, 313. Lists boys from a Brighton school who emigrated.

Petworth Emigration Committee

ABLETT, FREDA. 'Petworth Emigration Scheme', *B.R.L.H.S.N.* 24, 1991, 8-9. Lists emigrants to Canada from Bognor Regis area.

CAMERON, WENDY, & MAUDE, MARY MCDOUGALL. *Assisting emigration to Upper Canada: the Petworth project, 1832-1837.* McGill-Queens University Press, 2000.

CAMERON, WENDY. 'Petworth emigrants in Adelaide township: the cost of assisted emigration in 1832', *The London and Middlesex historian* 18, 1991, 18-31. This 'Adelaide' was in the district of London, Upper Canada; the journal is Canadian, not English.

CAMERON, WENDY, & MAUDE, MARY MCDOUGALL. *The Petworth Emigration Scheme: a preliminary list of emigrants from Sussex and neighbouring counties in England to Upper Canada 1832-1837.* Toronto: Wordforce, 1990.

CAMERON, WENDY. 'The Petworth Emigration Committee: Lord Egremont's assisted emigrations from Sussex to Upper Canada, 1832-1837', *Ontario history* 65(4), 1973, 231-46.

GOLDEN, JACQUELINE. 'The Petworth Emigration Society', *W.Sx.H.* **16**, 1980, 4-9.

LAWSON, LEIGH, & HAINES, SHEILA. 'A forest of family trees', *Sx.F.H.* **10**(6), 1993, 215-8. Originally published in *West Sussex history* 51, 1993. Discussion of research project on the Petworth Emigration Committee.

LAWSON, LEIGH, & HAINES, SHEILA. 'A forest of family trees', *W.Sx.H.* **51**, 1993, 14-17. Brief discussion of research on the Petworth Emigration Committee.

Australia

BARNES, ANDREW. 'Brede emigrants', *Sx.F.H.* **11**(7), 1995, 260. List of emigrants to Australia, 1838, found in the parish register.

BURCHALL, MICHAEL J. 'Sussex emigrants', *Sx.F.H.* **3**(6), 1978, 162-3. Lists emigrants to Australia and Canada in 1838-57.

BUTLER, C. 'Transportation & emigration from the Bognor area in the early 19th century', *B.R.L.H.S.N.* **5**, 1981, 7. Brief note.

COOPER, GLENNIS. 'Henry Dendy and his special survey', *R. & B.* **19**(2), 1992, 66-8; **19**(3), 1992, 92-5. With list of Surrey and Sussex settlers in Brighton, Victoria.

DAVEY, ROGER. ed. *East Sussex sentences of transportation at Quarter Sessions, 1790-1854.* Lewes: Friends of East Sussex Record Office, 1988.

HAM, JOAN. 'The West Sussex colonists', *W.Sx.H.* **34**, 1986, 5-11. Paupers from Sullington and Storrington, migrants to Western Australia.

JONES, KAREN. 'Dendy's emigrants', *E.Sy.F.H.S.J.* **14**(4), 1991, 26-9. Includes list of Surrey emigrants to Brighton, Victoria in 1842.

KING, FAY, & KING, ALBERT. 'Sussex to Sydney in the Neptune', *Sx.F.H.* **8**(2), 1988, 63-5. List of passengers from Salehurst area, 1839.

KING, FAY, & KING, ALBERT. 'Sussex to Sydney in the Neptune', *H. & R.F.H.S.J.* **3**(4), 1989, 76-80. List of emigrants from Salehurst and Hawkhurst area, 1839.

ROSER, BRIAN. 'Some Sussex women who strayed', *Sx.F.H.* **12**(1), 1996, 3-6; **12**(2), 1996, 49-52; **12**(3), 1996, 106-8; **12**(4), 1996, 150-55. Study of convicts transported to Australia.

New Zealand

HOAD, JOYCE. 'Were they discharged in New Zealand?', *E.Sy.F.H.S.J.* **17**(4), 1994, 21-3. Includes list of Surrey soldiers discharged in New Zealand.

HOAD, JOYCE. 'Were they discharged in New Zealand?', *Sx.F.H.* **11**(1), 1994, 27-9. Lists Sussex soldiers discharged in New Zealand, mid-19th c.

North America

DABNER, RALPH. 'The stay-together covenant of 1639', *R. & B.* **7**(2), 1980, 55-6. Covenant taken by emigrants from Surrey, *etc.,* to Guilford, Connecticut, in 1639 and 1650, with names.

BURCHALL, M.J. 'Parish-organized emigration to America: 19th century examples from East Sussex', *Genealogists magazine* **18**(7), 1976, 336-42. Based on records for Brede, Framfield and Hailsham, with many names of emigrants.

CAMERON, WENDY, HAINES, SHEILA, & MAUDE, MARY McDOUGALL. eds. *English immigrant voices: labourers letters from Upper Canada in the 1830s.* McGill-Queen's University Press, 2000.

CHALLEN, W.H. 'Sussex emigrants to America and West Indies', *Sx.N.Q.* **8**, 1940-41, 222-3. List, 1719-39 of Sussex 'certificates of agreement' to serve.

KAMINKOW, MARION, & KAMINKOW, JACK, eds. *Original lists of emigrants in bondage from London to the American colonies, 1719-44.* Baltimore: Magna Canta Book Co., 1967. Including many from Surrey.

STROUD, SARA PEARSON. 'The pauper shipment: *Nelson Wood,* 1837', *Sx.G.L.H.* **7**(3 & 4) 1986, 82-3. List of pauper emigrants from Alfriston, Eastbourne, Folkington, Jevington and Westham.

WALKER, RAYMOND. 'New York passenger list of 1828', *H. & R.F.H.S.J.* **10**(2), 1995, 38-9. Lists passengers embarking at Rye.

Excisemen

See Customs and Excisemen

Farmers

FARRANT, JOHN H. 'Spirited and intelligent farmers: the Arthur Youngs and the Board of Agriculture's reports on Sussex, 1793 and 1808', *Sx.A.C.* **130**, 1992, 200-212. Includes list of farmers whose practices were cited in the reports.

HARWOOD, B. 'Sussex agrarian historical records', *Sx.F.H.* **6**(1), 1984, 14-19. Bibliographical essay on sources for farmers, agricultural labourers, *etc.*

Fishermen

GEORGE, ANDREW, & FARRANT, JOHN. 'Brighton's fishermen in 1625', *Sx.G.L.H.* **7**(1), 1985, 4-6. Includes list.

REED, T. 'Eastbourne fishermen, pleasure boatmen, & lifeboatmen', *E.L.H.S.N.* **25**, 1977, 5-6. List, with nick-names, 18-19th c.

PEAK, STEVE. *Fishermen of Hastings: 200 years of the Hastings fishing community.* St. Leonards on Sea: News Books, 1985.

Flax Growers

CHAPMAN, A.M.J. 'Sussex flax yeilds in 1784', *Sx.F.H.* **13**(5), 1999, 177-8. Lists flax growers, 1784.

Footballers

Brighton & Hove Albion

CARDER, TIM, & HARRIS, ROGER. *Albion A-Z: a who's who of Brighton & Hove Albion F.C.* Brighton: Goldstone Books, 1997.

Crystal Palace

PURKISS, MIKE, & SANDS, NIGEL. *Crystal Palace: a complete record, 1905-1989.* Derby: Breedon Books Sports, 1990. Includes many brief biographies of footballers.

Dulwich Hamlet

A history of the Dulwich Hamlet Football Club, 1893/4-1967/8. [ ], 1968. Many names of footballers.

Old Alleynians

BLUNDELL, N.H. *Old Alleynian Rugby Football Club, 1898-1948.* William Clowes and Sons, 1949. Many names.

Richmond

EREAUT, E.J. *Richmond Football Club from 1861 to 1925.* Howlett & Son, 1926. Includes many names of footballers.

Woking

SHERLOCK, ROGER, & CUMMING, ROBERT. *Cardinal red: the history of Woking F.C.* Farnborough: CNR Sports Promotions, 1995. Includes 'career records' of players.

Freemasons

JOHNSTONE, JAMES. *History of the Lodge of Harmony no.255, 1785-1937, and Chapter of Iris no.255, 1807-1937.* G.Kenning & Sons, 1938. Freemasonry in Hampton, Richmond and Kew; includes list of 'members of lodge since 1785'.

The Richmond Lodge no.2032, founded 25th March 1884: record of fifty years. [Richmond]: the Lodge, 1934. Includes list of members.

Gamekeepers

SALZMAN, L.F. *Record of deputations of gamekeepers.* Sx.R.S. **51**. 1950. Lists manorial lords and their gamekeepers, 1781-1928 (but mainly prior to 1850).

Glass Makers

BOWLES, WILLIAM HENRY. *History of the Vauxhall and Ratcliff glasshouses and their owners, 1670-1800.* Privately published, 1926. Particularly useful for the Bowles family.

KENYON, G.H. *The glass industry of the Weald.* Leicester: Leicester University Press, 1967. General study; includes chapter on 'glassmaking families'.

WINBOLT, S.E. *Wealden glass: the old Surrey-Sussex industry. (A.D.1226-1615).* Hove: Combridges, 1933. Includes a few names of glassmakers.

Golfers

MILTON, ROSEMARY. *A history of Ladies golf in Sussex.* [ ]: Sussex Ladies Golf Association, 1993. Includes notes on 'some leading players and administrators in Sussex golf'.

Blackheath

HENDERSON, IAN T., & STIRK, DAVID I. *Royal Blackheath.* Henderson and Stirk, 1981. Golfing history; many golfers mentioned.

HUGHES, W.E. *Chronicles of Blackheath golfers.* Chapman & Hall, 1897. Identifies many 19th c. golfers.

Bognor Regis
BEALE, G. *Bognor Regis Golf Club 1892-1992: a centenary history.* Bognor Regis: the Club, 1992. Includes various lists of golfers.

Dulwich
BRENNAND, TOM. *Dulwich & Sydenham Hill the centenary history of a golf club; 1894-1994.* The Club, 1994. Includes lists of officers.

Farnham
DUNNE, NIGEL. *The history of Farnham Golf Club.* Farnham: the Club, 1996. Includes lists of the Club's presidents and captains since 1897. with many other names.

Hindhead
IRWIN-BROWN, RALPH. *Hindhead's turn will come; the unauthorized history of a golf club.* [ ]: the author, 1991. Includes many biographical notices of golfers.

Purley Downs
1894-1994 Purley Downs Golf Club: a centenary celebration. [Purley]: Purley Downs Colf Club 1994. Includes various lists of golfers.

Worthing
Worthing Golf Club 1905-1980: the story of the first seventy-five years. Worthing: Worthing Golf Club, 1980.

Gunfounders
LLOYD, CHRISTOPHER. 'Sussex guns', *History today* **23**, 1973, 785-91. Brief study of gunfounders, 16-18th c.

TOMLINSON, H.C. 'Wealden gunfounding: an analysis of its demise in the eighteenth century', *Economic history review* 2nd series **29**, 1976, 383-400. General study of Kent, Surrey and Sussex; includes some names of ironmasters.

Gunpowder Manufacturers
CROCKER, GLENYS, & CROCKER, ALAN. 'Gunpowder mills of Surrey', *Surrey history* **4**(3), 1990, 134-58. Includes 'list of Surrey gunpowder makers'.

WEST, JENNY. *Government, gunpowder and war in the mid-eighteenth century.* Studies in history **63**. Woodbridge: Boydell Press, for the Royal Historical Society, 1991. Includes notes on gunpowder mills at Chilworth, Ewell, and Molesey, in Surrey.

Gypsies
KEET-BLACK, JANET. *The Sussex gypsy diaries.* South Chailey: Romany & Traveller Family History Society, 1999. Lists of gypsies compiled by the police, 1898-1926.

KEET-BLACK, JANET. *Some travellers in the 1891 census.* [ ]: Romany & Traveller Family History Soceity, 1999. Circus, gypsies, showmen, tramps, traveller, vagrants; extracts from Cumberland, Durham, Northumberland, Westmorland, East Sussex, Kent, London.

Hockey Players
PEARCE, MICHAEL L. *Richmond Hockey Club: a history.* The Club, 1974. Pamphlet; includes chapter on 'Some outstanding members'.

Home Guardsmen
PEPPERALL, R.A. *Soldiers of the King: the story of the 53rd Surrey Battalion Home Guard.* Wells: Clare Son & Company, 1946. Includes roll of officers (on disbandment).

GEDDES, G.W. *The Guildford Home Guard.* Aldershot: Gale & Polden, [1945?] Includes list of the 4th Guildford Battalion in 1940.

ENGLEFIELD, W.A.D. *Limpsfield Home Guard 1940-1945.* Whitefriars Press, 1946. Includes roll.

Hop Growers
HENDERSON, ALAN C. *Hop takers of Kent and Sussex and their issuers.* Spink, 1990. Includes list of issuers, with pedigrees of Austen and Pinyon, 18-19th c.

Horsemen
The Royal Horse Show ... annual horse show to be held at Richmond, Surrey ... Richmond: Royal Horse Show, 1892- . Includes innumerable names of horsemen.

Horticulturalists
See Botanists and Nurserymen

Huntsmen

ONSLOW, EARL OF. 'Hunting in Surrey',
Sy.A.C. **43**, 1935, 1-15.

REES, SIMON. *The Charlton hunt: a history.*
Chichester: Phillimore & Co., 1998.
Includes list of members of the hunt.

SALZMAN, L.F. 'The Harting park in 1714',
Sx.N.Q. **15**, 1958-62, 147-8. List of hounds
boarded out, with names of persons
boarding them.

Immigrants

See Ironmasters & Men

Innkeepers, Licencees, etc.

BAX, A. RIDLEY. 'The old taverns of Surrey',
Sy.A.C. **19**, 1906, 195-9. List of taverns,
with names of innkeepers.

MARTIN, DAVID. 'Alehouses and social control
in early seventeenth century West Sussex',
W.Sx.H. **56**, 1995, 13-18. See also 57, 1996,
31-2. General discussion.

HUNTER, JUDITH. 'Surrey inns licenced by
Sir Giles Mompesson, 1618-1620', *R. & B.*
14(4), 1988, 142. Lists licencees.

SAWYER, FREDERICK E. 'Sussex tavern-
keepers and taverns in 1636', *Sx.A.C.* **33**,
1883, 272-3. Brief list.

WOODEN, TERRY. 'Public houses, publicans
and other inhabitants of Surrey in 1805',
R. & B. **24**(1), 1997, 18-19. Lists publicans,
etc., tenants of Thomas Cooper in 1800.

CALDECOTT, J.B. 'Sussex taverns in 1636',
Sx.A.C. **79**, 1938, 61-73. Includes lists of
innkeepers.

Camberley
See Frimley

Croydon
JAMES, T.M. 'The inns of Croydon, 1640-1840',
Sy.A.C. **68**, 1971, 109-29. General history.

Danehill
WHITTICK, CHRISTOPHER. 'The history of the
Sheffield Arms', *D.P.H.S.M.* **6**(2), 1998, 1-
11. At Danehill; includes list of tenants, i.e.
innkeepers, 1779-1965.

Dorking
WOODEN, TERRY. 'Some old Dorking inns',
Dorking history **19**, 1998, 17-18. Includes
names of innkeepers from an Act of
Parliament, 1807.

East Grinstead
LEPPARD, M.J. 'The Rose and Crown',
Bulletin of the East Grinstead Society **30**,
1981, 10-11. In East Grinstead. Lists
innkeepers, 18-20th c.

Farnham
MARLOW, MAURICE. 'Farnham inns and
innkeepers of the 17th century',
F.M.S.Q.N. **10**(1), 1993, 10-15.

MARLOW, MAURICE. 'Hops, inns, and public
houses of Farnham during the 18th
century', *F.M.S.Q.N.* **10**(6), 1994, 113-24.
Primarily a list of inns, with some names
of innkeepers.

MARLOW, MAURICE. 'Inns, taverns and public
houses of Farnham during the 16th
century', *F.M.S.Q.N.* **11**(5), 1997, 94-5.
Includes names of innkeepers.

Fetcham
BLAIR, R.W.J. 'The old Rising Sun, Fetcham',
P.L.D.L.H.S. **4**(5), 1981, 126-33. Includes
'list of customary tenants', and 'list of
known occupiers'.

Frimley
CLARKE, KEN. *Time gentlemen please: the
history of licensed premises in Frimley
and Camberley prior to 1950.* [ ], [199-?].
Includes lists of licensees.

Lewes
G., W.H. 'Election expenses, Lewes, 1727:
account of money expended at the several
inns in Lewes', *Sx.N.Q.* **2**, 1929, 58-60.
Gives names of innkeepers, *etc.*

Southwark
CORNER, GEORGE R. 'On some of the ancient
inns of Southwark', *Sy.A.C.* **2**, 1864, 50-81.
Includes some names of innkeepers.

HART, W.H. 'Further remarks on some of the
ancient inns of Southwark', *Sy.A.C.* **3**,
1865, 193-207.

NORMAN, E. PHILIP. 'The Tabard Inn,
Southwark, The Queens Head, William
Rutter and St. Margarets church', *Sy.A.C.*
13, 1897, 28-38. Discussion of a lease of
1538.

RENDLE, WILLIAM, & NORMAN, PHILIP. *The
inns of old Southwark and their
associations.* Longmans Green & Co., 1888.
Includes will of John Mabb, 1578.

Walton

MARTIN, A.G. *Inns & taverns of Walton & Weybridge: some notes on their history.* Walton & Weybridge Local History Society paper **12**. 1974. Many names of innkeepers.

Weybridge

See Walton

Wandsworth

DIVINE, J.M. 'Licenced houses in Wandsworth 1786, *E.Sy.F.H.S.J.* **17**(1), 1994, 38. List of licensees.

West Brixton Hundred

RIDOUT, MAUREEEN. 'Not 76 trombones, but 76 public houses', *E.Sy.F.H.S.J.* **17**(2), 1994, 31-2. Discussion of the records of West Brixton Hundred brewster sessions 1786-1820, with notes on licensing.

Westham

LEWIS, MARIE. 'The Corporation Arms and Railway Hotel, Westham', *E.L.H.S.N.* **70**, 1988, 12-14. Includes list of licensees, 1855-1960, *etc.*
See also Brewers

Inventors

See Scientists

Ironmasters & Men

The iron industry was important in the Weald, 15-18th c. There are two general accounts of its history:

CLEERE, HENRY. & CROSSLEY, DAVID. *The iron industry of the Weald.* 2nd ed., edited by Jeremy Hodgkinson. Cardiff: Merton Priory Press, 1995. General history, with many names of ironmasters, *etc.*

STRAKER, ERNEST. *Wealden iron: a monograph on the former ironworks in the counties of Sussex, Surrey and Kent, comprising a history of the industry from the earliest times to its cessation, together with a topographical survey of the existing remains from personal observation.* G. Bell & Sons, 1931. Facsimile reprint, Newton Abbot: David & Charles, 1969. Includes many names of ironmasters.

For sources, see:

JACK, SYBIL M. 'Sources for the history of the Wealden iron industry in the Public Record Office', *Wealden iron: bulletin of the Wealden Iron Research Group* **17**, 1980, 12-14; 2nd series **1**, 1981, 7-10; **2**, 1982, 21-30; **3**, 1983, 25-32.

PHILLIPS, BRIAN. 'References to ironworks in records at the Sussex Record Offices', *Wealden iron: bulletin of the Wealden Iron Research Group* 2nd series **5**, 1985, 41-4.

Iron works accounts give many names of persons associated with the industry. See:

CROSSLEY, D.W., ed. *Sidney iron works accounts, 1542-1573.* Camden 4th series **5**. Royal Historical Society, 1975.

CROSSLEY, D.W. 'Ralph Hogge's ironworks accounts, 1576-81', *Sx.A.C.* **112**, 1974, 48-79. Includes many payments to woodcutters, also to other suppliers and workers, *etc.*

Many immigrants came to work in the iron industry, and a number of articles relating to them are available:

AWTY, BRIAN G. 'Aliens in the ironworking areas of the Weald: the subsidy rolls 1524-1603', *Wealden iron: bulletin of the Wealden Iron Research Group* 2nd series **4**, 1984, 13-78. Lists aliens in Sussex, Kent and Surrey, assumed to be ironworkers.

AWTY, B.G. 'Denization returns and lay subsidy rolls as sources for French ironworkers in the Weald', *Wealden iron: bulletin of the Wealden Iron Research Group* **13**, 1978, 17-19. 16th c.

AWTY, BRIAN. 'French immigrant ironworkers in Sussex 1541-44', *Sx.G.L.H.* **2**(3), 1980, 102-10.

AWTY, BRIAN G. 'Provisional identifications of ironworkers among French immigrants listed in the denization rolls of 1541 and 1544', *Wealden iron: bulletin of the Wealden Iron Research Group* **16**, 1979, 2-11.

PETTITT, JOSEPH. 'Aliens in Wealden iron districts 1524-5', *W.I.R.G.Bulletin* **3**, 1972, 11-14.

TURNBULL, J.M. 'Iron idustry in the Weald', *Sx.F.H.* **9**(4), 1990, 144-7. Includes list of 'immigrant ironworkers c.1490-1544', from denization rolls.

Other works on the industry include:

GORING, J.J. 'Wealden ironmasters in the age of Elizabeth', in IVES, E.W., KNECHT, R.J., & SCARISBRICK, J.J., eds. *Wealth and power in Tudor England: essays presented to S.T.Bindoff.* Athlone Press, 1978, 204-27. Includes list of 61 ironmasters.

HODGKINSON, J.S. 'Forges in the late eighteenth century Weald', *Wealden iron: bulletin of the Wealden Iron Research Group* 2nd series **17**, 1997, 13-23. Lists forges and their occupiers (i.e., iron masters)

LOWER, MARK ANTONY. 'Historical and archaeological notices of the iron works of the County of Sussex', *Sx.A.C.* **2**, 1849, 169-220. See also **3**, 1850, 240-8. Includes many names of iron masters.

LOWER, MARK ANTONY. 'Historical and archaeological notices of the ironworks of the County of Sussex', *Wealden iron: bulletin of the Wealden Iron Research Group* **10**, 1976, 1-35. Reprinted from *Sx.A.C.* **2**, 1849, 169-220.

STRAKER, ERNEST. 'Wealden ironworks in 1574', *Sx.N.Q.* **7**, 1938-9, 97-103. Lists ironmasters of Sussex and Kent.

'Wealden iron: the Petworth connection', *Petworth Society magazine* **81**, 1995, 29-34. Brief note.

See also Gunfounders

Labourers

GOWER, MARION. *Bognor's early labourers and domestics (1841-1871).* Bognor Regis: Bognor Regis Local History Society, 2000.

GOWLER, MICHAEL A.H. *Labourers and domestics in Bognor (1841-1871): an analysis of names and numbers.* Bognor Regis: Bognor Regis Local History Society, 2000. Based on the census.

See also Agricultural Labourers.

Lawyers

BAX, ALFRED RIDLEY. 'Members of the Inner Temple, 1547-1660, and masters of the bench of the Hon. Society of the Inner Temple, 1450-1883, who, by birth, residence, office, &c., have been connected with the County of Surrey', *Sy.A.C.* **14**, 1899, 19-41. List with biographical notes.

NEWMAN, RONALD. 'Sussex lawyers in 1839', *Sx.F.H.* **11**(7), 1995, 255-6. List from *Pigot's directory*

Lifeboatmen

WILSON, BARRY. 'Lifeboat tragedy at Rye Harbour', *H.& R.F.H.S.J.* **9**(1), 1994, 6. List of lifeboatmen lost in 1928.

Literary Men

BELLAMY, C.H. 'Literati of Sussex', *Papers of Manchester Literary Club* **57**, 1931, 166-86. Brief biographies of literary men.

Masons

See Building Tradesmen

Medical Practitioners, *etc.*

FOSTER, JANET. 'Hospital records in the Greater London Record Office', *Genealogists magazine* **24**(3), 1992, 93-5. Includes list of records from hospitals in metropolitan Surrey.

Kelly's London medical directory. 7 issues, Kelly & Co., 1889-95. Covers metropolitan Surrey north of Croydon, and lists many allied professions e.g. coroners, surgical instrument makers, etc.

RIPMAN, H.A., ed. *Guy's Hospital, 1725-1948.* Guys Hospital Gazette Committee, 1951. Includes lists of various officers.

CAMERON, H.C. *Mr. Guy's Hospital, 1726-1948.* Longman Green & Co., 1954. Includes list of senior staff, etc. Extensive.

GREEN, J.K. *Sidelights on Guildford history 4: some Guildford doctors during the nineteenth century, the families of Newland, Eager, Sells, Stedman and Taylor.* Surrey Times, 1956. Originally published in the *Surrey Times.*

LYLE, H. WILLOUGHBY. *Kings and some King's men, being a record of the Medical Department of King's College, London, from 1830 to 1909, and of King's College Hospital Medical School, from 1909 to 1934.* Oxford University Press, 1935. Continued by Lyle's *An addendum to Kings and some King's Men (London) being an added record ... to 5 July 1948.* Oxford University Press, 1950. The college moved to Denmark Hill in 1913. Includes various lists of names and much biographical information.

GALLAGHER, SHEILA. 'Westminster/General Lying-in Hospital 1767-1971: history and records', *E.Sy.F.H.S.J.* **22**(1), 1999, 37-43; **22**(3), 1999, 29-42; **22**(4), 1999, 9-10. In Lambeth; many records relating to patients listed.

STEER, FRANCIS W. *The Royal West Sussex Hospital: the first hundred years, 1784-1884.* Chichester papers **15**. Chichester: Chichester City Council, 1960. Includes list of medical officers, 1826-84.

MCINNES, E.M. *St. Thomas' Hospital.* 2nd ed. Special Trustees for St. Thomas Hospital, 1990. Includes list of officers.

MCINNES, EILIDH M. 'St. Thomas's Hospital, London, and its archives', *Journal of the Society of Archivists* **1**(10), 1959, 277-82.

PARSONS, F.G. *The history of St. Thomas's Hospital.* 3 vols. Methuen & Co., 1932-6. Includes lists of officers.

BEAUFORT, D.A. 'The medical practitioners of Western Sussex in the early modern period: a preliminary survey', *Sx.A.C.* **131**, 1993, 139-51. General discussion of sources, *etc.*

Merchants

See Ship Owners & Masters, and Wool Merchants

Militiamen

SURREY

HORE, LIZ, & TAMBLIN, STUART. *Musters of the Surrey militia 1781-82.* 3 fiche. [ ]: Family History Indexes, 2000.

O'SULLIVAN, MAUREEN. 'Sir John Frederick's Company 1794', *E.Sy.F.H.S.J.* **11**(2), 1988, 39-40. List of a Surrey militia company.

Surrey musters (taken from the Loseley mss.). Sy.R.S. **3**. 1914-19. Published as nos. **2, 10, 11** & **13** of the Society's publications. 16-17th c.

Farnham

PARKS, R.N. 'Farnham papers: the militia', *F.M.S.Q.N.* **7**(1), 1984, 19-22. From the parish chest, mainly early 19th c.

Godalming

WEBB, CLIFF. 'The Godalming militia roll, 1759', *R. & B.* **8**(3), 1981, 107-8.

Wimbledon

O'SULLIVAN, MAUREEN. 'Wimbledon militia book, 1796', *E.Sy.F.H.S.J.* **12**(1), 1989, 35-6.

O'SULLIVAN, MAUREEN. 'Wimbledon Militia', *E.Sy.F.H.S.J.* **12**(2), 1989, 36. List from various sources, c.1790-1811.

SUSSEX

HORE, LIZ, & TAMBLIN, STUART. *Musters of the Sussex militia, 1781-82.* [ ]: Family History Indexes, 2000.

CHAPMAN, A.M.J. 'Sussex Militia deserters', *Sx.F.H.* **13**(7), 1999, 225-32. Lists for 1820 and 1821 from the *Sussex weekly advertiser.*

Burwash

MESLEY, ROBERT. 'Officers of the 2nd Royal Surrey Militia 1759-1876', *R. & B.* **26**(4), 2000, 154-5. To be continued. List.

Burwash, Pevensey & Rottingdean militia lists 1810, 1831, 1797. Eastbourne: PBN Publications 1992.

Eastbourne

BURCHALL, MICHAEL J. 'Eastbourne men at war in 1803: a census of male inhabitants aged 17-55', *Sx.G.L.H.* **6**(1), 1984, 25-31. Lists 338 men.

Icklesham

'Icklesham men at war in 1803: a census of male inhabitants aged 17-55', *Sx.G.L.H.* **7**(2), 1985, 51-2. Lists men liable to serve in the militia.

Pevensey

See Burwash

Pevensey Rape

Sussex militia list, Pevensey Rape, 1803: Northern Division. Eastbourne: PBN Publications, 1988.

Sussex militia list 1803: Southern Division, Pevensey Rape. Eastbourne: PBN Publications, 1988.

'Sussex militia', *F.R.* **11**(4), 1997, 80. List of deserters, Pevensey Rape, 1820, from the *Sussex advertiser.*

Rottingdean

See Burwash

Millers

BRUNNARIUS, MARTIN. *Windmills of Sussex.* Chichester: Phillimore, 1979. Gives names of millers, *etc.*

FARRIES, K.G., & MASON, M.T. *The windmills of Surrey and Inner London.* Charles Skilton, 1966. Gives names of millers, *etc.*

STIDDER, DEREK. *The watermills of Surrey.*
Buckingham: Barracuda, 1990. Primarily
a gazetteer; includes many names of
millers.

STIDDER, DEREK, & SMITH, COLIN.
Watermills of Sussex. 2 vols. [ ]: Baron
Birch, 1997-2000. v.1. East Sussex. v.2.
West Sussex.

PATERSON, D., *et al.* 'A bibliography of
Sussex mills', *Sussex industrial history*
22, 1992, 14-19.

Alfriston
COUPER, G.M. 'Berwick Windmill, Alfriston',
Sx.F.H. **10**(4), 1992, 145-6. Identifies
millers and millowners, 17-18th c.

Brighton
DAWES, H.T. *The windmills and millers of
Brighton.* Published as *Sussex industrial
history* **18**. 1988.

Crabtree
GILLAM, CLIFF. 'Two mills of West Sussex',
W.Sx.H. **61**, 1998, 27-36. At Mill Lane,
Crabtree; includes notes on millers.

East Grinstead
TIGHE, M.F. 'The mills of Forest Row', *Sussex
industrial history* **23**, 1993, 6-12. See also
24, 1994, 23-4. Includes list of millers in
the East Grinstead area, 1851.

Eastbourne
STEVENS, LAWRENCE. 'Mills of the
Eastbourne Borough Council area',
E.L.H.S.N. **38**, 1980, 3-9. List, with names
of some millers.

STEVENS, LAWRENCE. 'Mills of the
Eastbourne Borough Council area', *Sussex
industrial history* **27**, 1997, 22-9. Includes
list, with names of some millers.

Fishbourne
BLAKENEY, R. 'The mills at Fishbourne',
Sx.A.S.N. **26**, 1978, 162-6. Includes notes
on millers, medieval-19th c.

Lambeth
SHORT, MICHAEL. *Windmills in Lambeth: an
historical survey.* Lambeth Public
Libraries, 1971. Identifies many millers.

Lumley
YOWARD, TONY. 'Lumley Mill', *Sussex
industrial history* **24**, 1994, 30-36. Includes
names of millers, and list of employees
1906-14.

Wandsworth
G., A.E. *The mills and mealemen of
Wandsworth together with an interesting
account of some historical associations of
the River Wandle.* Boro' news
handbooks **1**. Wandsworth: Wandsworth
Boro' News Co., 1911. Includes list of
burials, wills, *etc.*, of 'mealemen', i.e.,
millers.

Warbleton
BESWICK, M. *Cornmills in and around
Warbleton.* Warbleton & District History
Group publication **12**. 1997. Many names of
millers.

Motor Manufacturers
CORKE, SHIRLEY. 'Dennis of Guildford: an
introduction to the firm and its records',
Surrey history **3**(3), 1986/7, 106-14. Motor
manufacturing firms; records include some
relating to personnel.

Murderers
EDDLESTON, JOHN J. *Murderous Sussex: the
executed of the twentieth century.* Derby:
Breedon Books, 1997.

LANE, BRIAN, ed. *The murder club guide to
South-East England.* Harrap, 1988. Covers
Surrey, Sussex, Kent and Hampshire.

TAYLOR, RUPERT. *Murders of old Sussex.*
Newbury: Countryside Books, 1991.

Musicians
FLANAGAN, BOB. *West Norwood Cemetery's
musicians.* Friends of West Norwood
Cemetery, 1998. 41 brief biographies.
See also Authors

Nurserymen
WILLSON, E.J. *Nurserymen to the world: the
nursery gardens of Woking and North-
West Surrey, and plants introduced by
them.* E.J.Willson, 1989. Includes many
names of nurserymen.
See also Botanists

Oddfellows

PAYNE, CHRISTINE. 'An old poster of the Oddfellows', *Sx.F.H.* **7**(2), 1986, 62-3. Lists the committee and stewards of a friendly society's Brighton branch, 1852.

Orphans

GORING, TONY. 'The Royal Female Orphanage: an intriguing cure', *E.Sy.F.H.S.J.* **18**(2), 1995, 32-6. See also **18**(3), 1995, 42. At Lambeth.

ROLPH, HARRY EDWARD. *The home on the hill.* [ ]: Reedham Old Scholars Association, 1981. History of Reedham Orphanage, subsequently Reedham School; includes 'list of marriages solemnized in the Aveling Memorial church, 1888-1965'.

Paper Makers

CROCKER, ALAN, 'The paper mills of Surrey', *Surrey history* **4**(1), 1989/90, 49-64; **4**(4), 1992, 211-30; **5**(1), 1994, 2-23.

SHORTER, ALFRED H. 'Paper-mills in Sussex', *Sx.N.Q.* **13**, 1950-53, 169-74. List, with many names of paper makers.

CROCKER, ALAN. *Paper mills of the Tillingbourne: a history of paper making in a Surrey valley, 1704 to 1875.* Oxshott: Tabard Private Press, 1988. Includes 'list of paper makers'.

CROCKER, ALAN. 'Watermarks in Surrey hand-made paper', *Surrey history* **3**(1), 1984-5, 2-16. Includes list of 'makers of Surrey hand-made paper', 18-19th c.

Photographers

LEPPARD, M.J. 'Early photographers in East Grinstead', *Sussex history* **1**(4), 1977, 29-31. Brief note.

LEPPARD, M.J. 'Early photographers in East Grinstead', *Bulletin of the East Grinstead Society* **18**, 1976, 8-9. 19th c.

MUNCEY, FRANCES. 'Two early Eastbourne photographic firms', *E.L.H.* **108**, 1998, 11-16. Vidler and Lavis families, 19-20th c.

MUNCEY, FRANCES. 'More photographers', *E.L.H.* 110 1998, 8-10. Notes on various photographers.

Pipemakers

ATKINSON, D.R. *Sussex clay tobacco pipes and the pipemakers.* Eastbourne: CRAIN Services, [197-]. Includes 'revised list of Sussex makers'.

ATKINSON, D.R. 'A new list of Sussex pipemakers', *Sx.A.C.* **110**, 1972, 37-43. 17-19th c.

ATKINSON, D.R. 'Sussex clay tobacco pipes and pipe makers', *Sx.N.Q.* **16**, 1963-7, 73-81 & 125-8. See also 170-72. List, 18-20th c.

ATKINSON, D.R. 'Further notes on Sussex clay tobacco pipes and pipemakers', *Sx.N.Q.* **16**, 1963-7, 272-6 & 312-7; **17**, 1968-71, 11-14. See also 61 & 104-5. Includes further lists of pipemakers, 17-19th c.

HIGGINS, DAVID. 'Surrey clay tobacco pipes', in DAVEY, PETER, ed. *The archaeology of the clay tobacco pipe VI: pipes and kilns of the London region.* British Archaeological reports **97**. 1981, 189-292. Includes 'provisional list of Surrey pipe-makers'.

Chichester

ATKINSON, D.R. 'Clay tobacco pipemakers of Chichester', *Sx.N.Q.* **17**, 1968-71, 158-61. 17-19th c.

Croydon

PEARMAN, K.R. 'Pipe makers of the Croydon region', *Proceedings of the Croydon Natural History and Scientific Society Ltd.* **16**(1), 1974, 23-4. Brief note.

Lewes

RECTOR, W.K. 'Pipemakers of Lewes in the 18th and 19th centuries', *Sx.N.Q.* **15**, 1958-62, 315-7. List.

Newington

TATMAN, COLIN ANDREW. *The Clay tobacco pipe industry in the parish of Newington, Southwark, London.* The archaeology of the clay tobacco pipe 13. B.A.R. British series **239**. Hadrian Books, 1994. Includes much biographical information, with pedigree of Swinyard and Critchfield, 18-19th c.

Southwark

WALKER, STEPHEN. 'The clay pipe industry in the parish of St. Olave's, Southwark', in DAVEY, PETER, ed. *The archaeology, of the clay tobacco pipe VI: pipes and kilns in the London region.* B.A.R. British series **97**. 1981, 173-82. Includes list of 83 pipemakers, 17-18th c.

Poachers

J., P.A. 'Deer poachers in Petworth Park, 1623', *Petworth Society bulletin* **16**, 1979, 17-22.

Policemen

ANGEL, K. *East Sussex police, 1840-1967.* Lewes: East Sussex Police, 1967. Commemoration pamphlet, with portraits of chief constables.

DIBLEY, JOHN. 'The development of policing in Uckfield', *Hindsight: the journal of the Uckfield & District Preservation Society* **2**, 1996, 42-50; **3**, 1997, 40-45.

DURRANT, A.J. *A short centenary history of the Surrey constabulary 1851-1951.* [ ], 1951. Includes photographic portraits.

HOBBS, DORIS C.H. 'The Croydon police, 1829-1840', *Croydon Natural History and Scientific Society Ltd. proceedings.* **17**(6), 1983, 141-52. Includes list of officers.

Policyholders

HARWOOD, BRIAN. 'Sussex village hisstory from insurance records', *Sx.G.L.H.* **6**(2), 1984, 58-62. Lists policy holders of the Imperial Fire Insurance Company, 1868-77, in the Herstmonceux area.

Postmasters

GREENWOOD, JEREMY. *The posts of Sussex: the Chichester branch, 1250-1840.* Reigate: the author, 1973. Includes many names of postmasters, *etc.*

SMITH, W.L.H., & ORCHARD, S.C. *The history of the Post Office in Lewes.* Derby: CEM Publications, 1992. Identifies postmasters.

VINER, G.A. *The postal history of Chichester, 1635-1900.* Chichester papers **47**. Chichester: Chichester City Council, 1965. Includes list of postmasters.

Potters

BAINES, JOHN MANWARING. *Sussex pottery.* [ ]: Fisher Publications, 1980. Includes topographical survey, with some names of potters.

BRITTON, FRANK. *London delftware.* Jonathan Horn, 1987. Includes list of 450 18th c. potters, including many in Southwark, Lambeth and Putney.

DAVIES, ISABEL. 'Seventeenth-century delftware potters in St.Olave's parish, Southwark', *Sy.A.C.* **66**, 1969, 11-31.

SCOTT, P. *Pottery in Lambeth: a select bibliography.* Lambeth Public Libraries, 1976.

Prison Officer

BLAKE, PAUL. 'Brixton female prison 1856', *E.Sy.F.H.S.J.* **14**(3), 1991, 11-12. List of 'principal officers and clerks'.

Prostitutes

KARRAS, RUTH MAZO. 'The regulation of brothels in later medieval England', *Signs* **14**, 1989, 399-433. Study of Southwark.

Racing Fraternity

ONSLOW, EARL OF. 'Racing in Surrey', *Sy.A.C.* **44**, 1936, 1-23.

Railway Contractors & Engineers

POPPLEWELL, LAWRENCE. *A gazetteer of the railway contractors and engineers of South East England, 1830-1914.* Ferndown: Melledgen Press, 1983.

Railway Directors, etc.

COURSE, EDWIN. ed. *Minutes of the board of directors of the Reading, Guildford and Reigate Railway Company.* Sy.R.S. **33**. 1987. For 1845-52; includes 'Select list of persons associated with the Reading, Guildford and Reigate Railway', with biographical notes.

Railway Passengers

GRANT. R.C. 'The Clayton Tunnel disaster', *Sx.F.H.* **11**(5), 1995, 171-4. Lists victims of a rail disaster in 1861.

Railwaymen

ADAMS. CAROLINE. *et al. Railways in West Sussex.* Local history mini-guides to sources **4**. Chichester: West Sussex County Council, 1996. Includes brief note on staff records.

BRACKPOOL, C. 'Brighton Railway', *Sx.F.H.* **8**(6), 1989, 270-71. List of staff awarded medals *etc.* in the First World War.

MILTON, F.R. *Index to people working on the London, Brighton & South Coast Railway taken from the census 1851-81, Eastbourne & District area (includes Hailsham, Hellingly, Westham and part of Seaford).* Eastbourne: Family Roots F.H.S. (Eastbourne & District), 1987.

Rebels/Rioters

BLAAUW, W.H. 'Inquests concerning the rebels of Sussex after the Barons' War', *Sx.A.C.* **6**, 1853, 215-22. 1265.

HARVEY, I.M.W. *Jack Cade's rebellion of 1450.* Oxford: Clarendon Press, 1991. The rebellion primarily affected Kent, Surrey, Sussex and Essex.

ORRIDGE, B.B. *Illustrations of Jack Cade's rebellion ...* John Camden Hotten, 1869. Includes lists of Cade's followers in Kent and Sussex; also folded pedigree of Cooke of Gidea Hall, Essex, 16-19th c.

POOLE, ERIC. *Followers of Jack Cade's rebellion, 1450, from Kent, Sussex, Essex, and Surrey.* Kent Family History Society record publication **39**. 1985.

COOPER, WILLIAM DURRANT. 'Participation of Sussex in Cade's rising, 1450', *Sx.A.C.* **18**, 1866, 17-36. See also 37-41. Includes list of men pardoned.

BAX, ALFRED RIDLEY. 'Suspected persons in Surrey during the Commonwealth', *Sy.A.C.* **14**, 1899, 164-89. Includes list, 1655, of suspected royalists.

GORING, JEREMY. 'The riot at Bayham Abbey, June 1525', *Sx.A.C.* **116**, 1978, 1-10. Includes list of rioters.

BRICKLEY, PETER. 'Swing rioters in West Sussex 1830-31', *Sx.G.L.H.* **2**(2), 1980, 53-62. Includes list of rioters prosecuted.

School Pupils and Teachers, *etc.*

A. General

The majority of our ancestors in the last few centuries attended school. Many of them will have had their names recorded in the registers, *etc.,* of schools, colleges, universities, and other educational establishments. Educational archives also record the names of innumerable teachers, school governors, benefactors, and others connected with education. For Surrey, educational archives are listed in the somewhat outdated, but not superseded:

POWELL, D.L. *Records of schools and other endowed institutions,* ed. Hilary Jenkinson. Guides to Surrey records **4**. Surrey County Council, 1930. Also issued as Sy.R.S. publication no. **31**.

For the records of schools in Metropolitan Surrey, see:

WEBB, CLIFF. *An index of London schools and their records.* Society of Genealogists, 1999. Includes listing of records for schools in Battersea, Bermondsey, Camberwell, Lambeth, Southwark and Wandsworth.

There are no equivalent works for Sussex. There are however, two brief articles of county-wide interest. Extensive information on Sussex schools in the eighteenth century is provided in:

CAFFYN, JOAN, ed. *Sussex schools in the 18th century: schooling provision, schoolteachers, and scholars.* Sx.R.S. **81**. 1998. Includes biographical dictionaries of 'Sussex schoolmasters and school-mistresses in the 18th century', and 'Sussex scholars of the 18th century', i.e. school children.

For 17th c. Sussex matriculations at Oxford University, see:

BLISS, PHILIP. 'Oxford matriculations, 1615-1640', *Sx.A.C.* **9**, 1857, 363-4. Brief list.

Catholic schoolmasters in Sussex are listed in:

MCCANN, TIMOTHY J. 'Catholic schoolmasters in Sussex 1558-1603: addenda and corrigenda to Beales' Catholic schoolmasters', *Recusant history* **12**, 1973-4, 235-7.

B. *Schools*

The list of individual school histories, registers, *etc.,* which follows is not intended to be comprehensive; rather, it aims to identify works which are directly relevant to genealogical research, i.e. which contain names. School registers are particularly valuable sources of genealogical information.

SURREY

Barnes
See St. Paul's School

Borough Road Normal College

BARTLE, G.F. 'Early applications by women candidates to the Borough Road Normal College', *History of Education Society bulletin* **18**, 1976, 35-41. Discussion of records, 1836-52.

BARTLE, G.F. 'Early applications for admission to the Borough Road Normal College', *History of Education Society bulletin* **14**, 1974, 31-40. Discussion of the records of a teacher training institution.

BARTLE, G.F. 'The records of Borough Road College', *History of Education Society bulletin* **13**, 1974, 4-9. Brief discussion of the records of an early teacher training college.

Camberwell

PEARSE, R.N. *The story of the Mary Datchelor School 1877-1977.* 2nd ed. Hodder & Stoughton, 1977. Include list of long service staff.

ALLPORT, D.H. *Camberwell Grammar School: a short history of the foundation, under royal charter, of Edward Wilson, clerk, in Camberwell in the County of Surrey, commonly called Wilsons Grammar School, including an account of the former Greencoat School.* Rev. ed. The Governors, 1964. Includes 'Appendix: extracts from the school register: lists of governors, masters, foundationers, and captains of school and games, *etc*'; also details of 'the school's books and records'.

ALLPORT, D.H. *A short history of Wilsons School.* 3rd ed. Wilsons School Charitable Trust, 1987. Includes various lists of names.

Caterham

BLOMFIELD, ERNEST DE C. *A century at Caterham 1884-1984.* Kiek & Read, 1983. Includes lists of teachers.

Charterhouse

The school moved to Godalming in 1872. Previous registers of the school in London are listed in my *Londoners occupations.*

GIRDLESTONE, F.W.K., HARDMAN, E.T., & TOD, A.H. *Charterhouse register 1872-1910.* 2nd ed. 2 vols. Chiswick Press, 1911.

JAMESON, E.M. *Charterhouse register ... 1872-1931.* 3rd ed. 2 vols. Guildford: Old Carthusian Club, 1932.

PARISH, W.D. *List of Carthusians, 1800 to 1879.* Lewes: Farncombe & Co., 1879. School register.

Cheam

PEEL, EDWARD. *Cheam School from 1645.* Gloucester: Thornhill Press, 1974. Includes detailed notes on families which have sent 6 or more boys to Cheam.

ROBERTS-WEST, MAUDE. 'Cheam School', *Genealogists magazine* **5**, 1929-31, 130-33 & 162-7.

Cranleigh

MEGAHEY, ALAN J. *A history of Cranleigh School.* Collins, 1983. General history.

Croydon

THORNHILL, LILIAN. 'School log books: their contribution to social history', *Proceedings and transactions of the Croydon Natural History and Scientific Society Ltd.* **15**, 1972-6, 141-59. Especially in Croydon.

MAGNUS, LAURIE. *The Jubilee book of the Girls Public Day School Trust Limited ... Croydon High School, 1874-1924.* 2 fiche. East Surrey F.H.S. record publication **60**. 1997. Reprint. Originally published Cambridge University Press, 1923. Includes lists of staff and old girls.

PERCY, F.H.G. *History of Whitgift School.* B.T.Batsford, 1976. General history, with detailed notes on sources, list of alumni, 1600-1800, lists of masters, chairmen of the governors and benefactors, notes on the Whitgift family heraldry, *etc.*

PERCY, F.H.G. *Whitgift School: a history.* 2nd ed. Croydon: Whitgift Foundation, 1991. Expanded and re-titled from 1st edition.

History of the Whitgift Grammar School, with a register of all Whitgiftians from 1871 to 1892. Croydon: W.D.Hayward, 1892. Extensive.

MASON, M.H.H. *The book of remembrance, and list of members serving with H.M.Forces, 1914-1919.* Pettitt Cox & Bowers, [1920]. From Whitgift Grammar School, Croydon.

School Pupils and Teachers *etc*. (*cont.*)
Dorking
SYKES, EDWIN. *Do better still: the story of Powell Corderoy School (formerly the Dorking British School) 1816 to 1989.* Dorking: Dorking Local History Group, 1989.

Dulwich College
BLANCH, WILLIAM HARNETT. *Dulwich College and Edward Alleyn: a short history of the foundation of God's Gift College at Dulwich, together with a memoir of the founder.* E.W.Allen, 1877.

CHANDLER, ARTHUR R. *Alleyn's: the first century.* Charles Skilton, 1983. Includes list of staff from 1867.

HODGES, SHEILA. *God's gift: a living history of Dulwich College.* Heinemann Educational Books, 1981. Includes bibliography.

YOUNG, WILLIAM. *The history of Dulwich College, down to the passing of the Act of Parliament dissolving the original corporation, 28th August, 1857, with a life of the founder, Edward Alleyn, and an accurate transcript of his diary 1617-1622, to which is added notices of the lives and writings of some of the masters and fellows, together with notes on local peculiarities and associations.* 2 vols. Edinburgh: Morrison & Gibb, 1889. v.2. includes extracts from Dulwich manorial court rolls, 14-17th c.

WARNER, GEORGE F. *Catalogue of the manuscripts and muniments of Alleyn's College of God's Gift at Dulwich.* Spottiswoode & Co., 1881.

BICKLEY, FRANCIS B. *Catalogue of the manuscripts of Alleyn's College of God's Gift at Dulwich, Second series.* College Governors, 1903.

DUNNETT, HARDING McGREGOR. *Eminent Alleynians.* Benenden: Neville & Harding, 1984. Biographies of 60 eminent old boys.

ORMISTON, THOMAS LANE. *Dulwich College register 1619 to 1926.* [Dulwich: Alleyn Club], 1926.

CHRISTISON, McC. *Dulwich College war record 1914-1919.* J.J.Keliher, 1923.

First list of old Alleynians serving in the forces, July 1940. Dulwich College, 1940.

CHRISTISON, McC. *Dulwich College war record 1939-1945.* Keliher, Hudson & Kearns, 1949.

East Grinstead
HILL, FRANK. *Sackville College (Hospitale sive collegium).* East Grinstead: Farncombe & Co., 1913. At East Grinstead. Includes information on wardens, *etc*.

Epsom College
SALMON, MICHAEL A. *Epsom College 1855-1980: the first 125 years.* Oxford: Oxprint, 1980. Includes biographical notes on eminent old boys, and on headmasters, masters, and the college council.

Epsom College register, from October 1855 to July 1905. Richard Clay & Sons, 1905.

Epsom College register from October 1855 to December 1924. Rev. ed. Bungay: Richard Clay & Sons, 1925.

THOMSON, T.R., ed. *Epsom College register, 1855-1954.* Oxford: University Press for the Old Epsomian Club, 1955.

Farnham
SPRING, LAWRENCE, & HALL, DEREK. *The Farnham Greencoats: Samuel Jones Regiment of Foot.* 2nd ed. Leigh on Sea: Partizan Press, 1988. Regiment raised in 1643; includes biographical notes on officers.

Godalming
See Charterhouse

Guildford
GREEN, J.K. *Sidelights on Guildford history III: some of the schools of Guildford. Charity schools; private day schools; boarding schools for ladies and young gentlemen.* Guildford: J.K.Green, 1954.

STURLEY, D.M. *The Royal Grammar School, Guildford.* Guildford: the School, 1980.

WILLIAMSON, G.C. *The Royal Grammar School of Guildford, 1509: a record and review.* G.Bell & Sons, 1929. Includes rent roll, 1671, wills of Robert & Elizabeth Beckingham, 1509-10, Thomas Polstead, 1528-9, & William Nettles, 1691, list of old boys, 1780-1818, *etc*.

Kennington

SILVER, PAMELA, & SILVER, HAROLD. *The education of the poor: the history of a National School, 1824-1874*. Routledge, 1974. History of Kennington Nation School, useful for its list of school records.

Lambeth

BROWNE, J. CAVE. *The history of the Lambeth Parochial Boys School, with a list of the treasurers, and a short account of the schoolmasters, and of the legacies and donations*. Lambeth: Buck & Wootton, 1851. Brief pamphlet.

WOOD, JOHN E., & GOODFELLOW, EDWIN H. *Old Lambethans, past and present: a tribute, with a history of the School*. Old Lambethan Society, 1907. Brief biographies of prominent old boys.

Leatherhead

DONALDSON, W.L., ed. *A register of St. Johns School, Leatherhead, 1852-1937*. Croydon: Roffey & Clark, [1938].

WILLIAMS, E.M.P. *The quest goes on, being a short history of the first hundred years of St. John's School, Leatherhead, 1851-1951*. Leatherhead: [ ], 1951. Includes 'Pro patria: a list of those who lost their lives on service in the South African war, the World Wars, and rebellions or mutinies'.

Putney

PIKE, MURIEL. *The Oak Tree: the story of Putney High School*. Brighton: Dolphin Press, 1960. Many names mentioned.

Richmond

CUMBERS, F.H., ed. *Richmond College 1843-1943*. Epworth Press, 1944. Methodist theological training college; includes 'list of students, 1843-1940'.

St.Paul's

MEAD, ARTHUR H. *St. Paul's School registers*. St. Paul's School, 1990. Now at Barnes. This volume covers 1905-85. For earlier registers, see Raymond's *Londoners Occupations*.

Sheen

See Temple Grove

Shirley

ADAMS, J.A.D., & COLL, GERRY. *The history of Shirley Oaks Childrens Home*. Deptford Forum Publishing, 1999. At Shirley, 20th c. Includes autobiographical accounts of former children.

Southwark

CARRINGTON, R.C. *Two schools: a history of the St. Olave's and St. Saviour's Grammar School Foundation*. The Governors, 1971. Southwark schools; includes lists of headmasters and wardens; also note on Harvard family, 17-20th c.

A list of patrons on the anniversary of the Charity-Schools, MDCCCXLII. Norris & Son, 1842. Extensive listing, with addresses. The charity schools concerned are those of London, Westminster, Southwark and environs.

Temple Grove

WATERFIELD, H.W. *Temple Grove register*. [ ], 1905. School at Sheen; 19th c. register.

WRIGHT, SIMON. *Waterfield's School: a preparatory school in its Victorian heyday*. Heron's Ghyll Press, [199-]. Includes brief biographies of 100 old boys.

Walton

LE FEVRE, MARGARET. *300 years of local schools*. Walton & Weybridge Local History Society paper 5. 1970.

Wandsworth

SCOTT-GILES, C.W. *The history of Emanuell School, 1594-1964*. Old Emanuel Association, 1977. The school moved from Westminster to Wandsworth in 1883.

Weybridge

See Walton

Willington

KLAUS, MARX. *My first and best school: Willington School: the first hundred years*. Trustees of Willington School, 1985. Many names.

Wimbledon

POOLE, ANTHONY. *A history of Wimbledon College*. Wimbledon College, 1992. Includes various lists of names. The College was founded in 1892.

School Pupils and Teachers *etc.* (*cont.*)
SUSSEX

Ardingly
ARGENT, NIGEL. *Ardingly College, 1939-1990.*
Autolycus Press, 1991. Includes roll of
honour 1939-45, list of staff, and many
other names.

A register of St. Saviour's School, Ardingly.
Oxford: Alden & Co., 1913.

Bognor Regis
LEE, JUDITH M. 'The bankrupt head teachers
of Bognor', *B.R.L.H.S.N.* **15**, 1986, 16-23.
19th c.

LEE, JUDITH M. 'Private schools in Bognor
Regis, 1880-1960', *B.R.L.H.S.N.* **7**, 1982, 9-
12. Brief discussion.

'A curious memorial', *B.R.L.H.S.N.* **8**, 1983, 8.
Memorial to boys at Middleton School,
Bognor Regis in 1885, with names.

Brighton
TIBBLE, RONALD. 'Schooling in Brighton
before the first Elementary Education Act
of 1870', *Sx.G.L.H.* 5(1), 1983, 4-12.

BURSTOW, G.P., & WHITTAKER, M.B. *A
history of Brighton College.* Brighton: the
College, 1957. Many names.

JONES, MARTIN D.W. *Brighton College, 1845-
1995.* Chichester: Phillimore, 1995. Many
names.

MATHEWS, H.J. *Brighton College register.
Part 1. 1847-1863. Nos.1-1000, with brief
biographical notices.* Brighton:
J.Farncombe, 1886.

MILLIKEN, E.K. *Brighton College register
1847-1922. Nos. 1-5000. With brief
biographical notes.* Brighton: Farncombe's,
1922. Supplemented by:

MILLIKEN, E.K. *Brighton College register
1847-1922: revisal and supplement.* 2
issues. Oxford: privately printed, 1923-5.

ASSOCIATION OF OLD BRIGHTONANS. *List of
members.* [Brighton]: the Association,
1919. There may be other issues.

Brighton College war record 1914-1919.
Brighton: Farncombes, 1920. Roll of
honour, with portraits.

Chichester
FAIRBROTHER, C.BURTON. *The Oliver Whitby
School at Chichester in the County of
Sussex: a brief account.* Chichester: Moore
& Taylor, 1956. Brief; includes note on
Oliver Whitby, 17th c.

Christs Hospital
ALLAN, G.A.T. *Christ's Hospital.* Rev ed. Ian
Allan, 1949.

PEARCE, E.H. *Annals of Christs Hospital.*
Methuen, 1901.

Christ's Hospital: four hundred years old.
Christ's Hospital, 1953. Record of
quartocentenary celebrations, with
historical & biographical notes on its
foundation.

Eastbourne
ALLOM, V.M. *Ex oriente salus: a centenary
history of Eastbourne College.*
Eastbourne: Eastbourne College, 1967.
Includes various lists of names.

MERRITT, E.D. *A history of Eastbourne
College.* Eastbourne: V.T.Sumfield, 1897.
Many names.

HODSOLL, V. 'The Grange, Eastbourne',
E.L.H.S.N. **36**, 1980, 3-6. Brief notes on a
school, and on the Hollins family, 19-20th c.

Hastings
BAINES, J. MANWARING, & CONISBEE, L.R.
*The history of Hastings Grammar School,
1619-1956.* Hastings: Hastings Grammar
School Foundation, 1956. Many names
mentioned.

Hurstpierpoint
JOHNSON, H.L. *Register of St. John's College,
Hurstpierpoint.* [Hurstpierpoint]: the
School, 1914. Covers 1849-1914.

KING, PETER. *Hurstpierpoint College 1849-
1995: the school by the Downs.* Chichester:
Phillimore & Co., 1997. Many names.

Lancing
WHITAKER, CUTHBERT W. ed. *A register of
St. Nicholas College, Lancing, from its
foundation at Shoreham in August,
MDCCCXLVIII to the commencement of
the month of November MDCCCC.*
Bradbury Agnew & Co., 1900.

GORDON, E.B., ed. *The Lancing register.* 3rd
ed. Cambridge: University Press, 1933.
Covers 1848-1932; includes roll of honour
1914-19, list of masters, and various other
appendices.

GORDON, E.B., ed. *The Lancing register ...
1901-1954.* 4th ed. Hove: Hove Shirley
Press, 1955.

*The calendar of St. Nicholas College,
Shoreham, for the year of our Lord ...*
Shoreham: Allever Butler, 1850-57.
Continued as *The calendar of the College
of S. Nicolas, Lancing, for the year of
Our Lord ...* 1858-9. There may be other
issues. These volumes include lists of staff
and boys, *etc.*

The Lancing roll of honour 1914-1919.
Medici Society, 1924. List of old Lancing
boys who served; includes portraits.

Midhurst
ROWE, E.F. *A history of Midhurst Grammar
School, with biographical notices of old
Midhurstians.* Hove: Combridge, 1913. Not
seen.

Steyning
BREACH, WILLIAM POWELL. 'Wm. Holland,
Alderman of Chichester, and the Steyning
Grammar School', *Sx.A.C.* **43**, 1900, 59-83.
Includes folded pedigree of Holland, 16-
17th c., wills of William Holland, 1614,
and various members of his family, also of
John Parson of Steyning, 1647, deeds, *etc.*

Uckfield
WRIGHT, S. *Payment by results: Uckfield
parochial school, 1863-1895.* Uckfield:
Uckfield & District Preservation Society,
1991.

Wadhurst
ASCOTT, KENNETH F. *The education of
Wadhurst.* Sussex: Book Guild, 1998.
School history; many names.

Wisborough Green
SARGENT, LIZ. *A history of Wisborough
Green School, 1850-1990.* [Wisborough
Green]: [ ], 1990. Includes list of staff.

Scientists
CAMPBELL, IRENE, HAYES, MARTIN, &
O'NEILL, MARTIN. *Scientists and inventors
in West Sussex.* Chichester: West Sussex
County Council, 1996. Brief biographical
dictionary.

Seamen
CHEAL, HENRY. *The ships and mariners of
Shoreham.* F.M.Bkake, 1909. Reprinted
Shoreham: G.E. & P.P.Bysh, 1981. Includes
list of master mariners, 1814-1909.

HOTHERSALL, MARJORIE. 'A note on West
Sussex shipping records', *W.Sx.H.* **52**,
1993, 7-9. Discussion of crew lists from
Arundel Chichester, Littlehampton and
Shoreham, late 19th c.

*Crew members of ships trading from
Newhaven, Sussex between 1864 & 1889.*
Eastborne: PBN Publications, 1990. Lists
from crew 'agreements'.

See also Ship Owners & Masters

Seamen (Royal Navy)
PHILP, ROY. *The coast blockade: the Royal
Navy's war on smuggling in Kent & Sussex,
1817-31.* Horsham: Compton Press, 1999.

'Men raised for the navy 1795-6',
Wandsworth notes and queries **11**, 1899,
220-21. List.

*Sussex enrolments under the Navy Acts,
1795 & 1797.* Eastbourne: PBN
Publications, 1992.

Servants
EBURY, M., & PRESTON, B. *Domestic service
in late-Victorian and Edwardian England,
1871-1914.* Geographical papers **42**.
Reading: University of Reading Dept. of
Geography, 1976. Partly based on 1871
census for Hastings, Lincoln, and parts of
Lancashire, Berkshire and Warwickshire.

SHORT, BRIAN. 'The decline of living-in
servants in the transition to capitalist
farming: a critique of the Sussex evidence',
Sx.A.C. **122**, 1984, 147-64. See also **123**,
1985, 225-41. General study.

Shepherds
WILLS, BARCLAY. *Shepherds of Sussex.*
Skeffington & Son, [1932]. Names from
this book are listed in:

HARWOOD, B. 'Sussex shepherds', *Sx.F.H.* **5**(5),
1983, 142-3.

Ship Owners & Masters
HEARN, J. RUDLAND. 'Sussex shipping
visiting the Liberty of the Water Thamer
in 1760-1761', *Sx.N.Q.* **16**. 1963-7, 231-3. i.e.
Plymouth area. Lists masters.

Arundel
HULME, E. WYNDHAM. 'Portbooks and
customs accounts of Arundel &
Littlehampton in the Tudor period',
Sx.N.Q. **9**, 1942-3, 106-8. Extracts naming
16th c. ships masters, *etc.*

Chichester

PELHAM, R.A. 'Sussex wool ports in the thirteenth century', *Sx.N.Q.* **5**, 1934-5, 101-3, 137-41 & 166-71. Lists ships masters and merchants at Chichester, Shoreham and Seaham.

PELHAM, R.A. 'The wool trade of Chichester, 1377-80', *Sx.N.Q.* **6**, 1936-7, 201-4. Accounts listing ships masters and merchants.

Hastings
See Rye

Littlehampton
See Arundel

Newhaven

FARRANT, JOHN H. 'Shipowning at Newhaven in the later 19th century', *Sussex industrial history* **8**, 1978, 17-23. Lists shipwoners.

Rye

HORNER, RICHARD. 'Rye and Hastings built or owned ships, from *Lloyds shipping register,* 1835', *H & R.F.H.S.J.* 3(1), 1988, 17-19. Lists ships masters and owners.

DELL, RICHARD F., ed. *Rye shipping records, 1566-1590.* Sx.R.S. **64**. 1966.

Seaham
See Chichester

Shoreham

PARKES, A.S. 'From York River to Yorkshire coast: the life & death of the Shoreham ship Nelson', *Sx.F.H.* 4(9), 1981, 295-99. Lists owners and masters, mid-19th c.

See also Chichester

Shipwrights

RIDGE, C. HAROLD. *Records of the Worshipful Company of Shipwrights, being an alphabetical digest of freemen and apprentices, &c.* 2 vols. Phillimore & Co., 1939-46. v.1. 1428 to 1780. v.2. 1728 to 1858. Many shipwrights listed had addresses on the South Bank.

Showmen, *etc.*

BLEACH, JOHN. 'Fairfield folk at Bodiam and Rudgwick fairs,'1841', *Sx.A.C.* **128**, 1990, 266-70. Census schedules listing showmen, dealers, *etc.*

Smugglers

DOUCH, JOHN. *Smuggling: the wicked trade.* Dover: Crabwell Publications/Buckland Publications, 1980. Includes much information on the Ransley family of Ruckinge.

WAUGH, MARY. *Smuggling in Kent and Sussex, 1700-1840.* Newbury: Countryside Books, 1985. Includes lists of smugglers.

WEBB Graham. 'Sussex smugglers: heroes or criminals', *Sx.G.L.H.* 2(3), 1980, 94-8. General discussion.

See also Customs & Excisemen

Soldiers

A. Medieval-19th c.

C., W., ed. 'Muster roll for the Rape of Hastings 13 Edw.III', *Collectanea topographica et genealogica* **7**, 1841, 118-28.

COOPER, WILLIAM DURRANT. 'Sussex men at Agincourt', *Sx.A.C.* **15**, 1863, 123-37. Includes lists.

BAX, ALFRED RIDLEY. 'Muster rolls of troops raised in Surrey to be employed in the Low Countries, 1627', *Sy.A.C.* **10**, 1891, 280-82. Lists 100 footmen.

HUDSON, ANN. 'Volunteer soldiers in Sussex during the Revolutionary and Napoleonic wars, 1793-1815', *Sx.A.C.* **122**, 1984, 165-81. General study.

BUTT, C.R. 'Volunteer force in Surrey, 1799-1813', *Journal of the Society for Army Historical Research* **40**, 1962, 207-13. Includes names of officers.

Sussex, Hampshire, Surrey & Kent: War Office list 1804: list of officers of the Gentlemen and Yeomanry Cavalry and Volunteer Infantry. Eastbourne: PBN Publications, 1995.

GIUSEPPI, M.S. 'Records relating to Surrey regiments', *Sy.A.C.* **27**, 1914, 150-54. Lists numerous muster rolls, *etc.,* at the Public Record Office.

B. *1st World War*

OLIVE, M.F. 'Autographs of wounded soldiers 1914-1918', *Sx.F.H.* **14**(1), 2000, 20-21. List from an autograph book.

LEWIS, MARIE. 'St. Mary's Hospital, Eastbourne', *F.R.* 4(3), 1990, 62-5. Lists soldiers who died in this military hospital, 1916-19.

MESLEY, BOB. *Surrey soldiers died in the Great War, 1914-1919.* Microfiche series **27**. West Surrey F.H.S., 1999.

MESLEY, ROBERT. 'Surrey soldiers died in the Great War, 1914-1919', *R. & B.* **26**(3), 1999, 117. Brief list of deaths in 1st Battalion Queens (Royal West Surrey Regiment).

IMPERIAL WAR GRAVES COMMISSION *The war dead of the commonwealth: the register of the names of those who fell in the first world war and are buried in the cemeteries and churchyards of the administrative county of East Sussex.* The commission, 1.931. Reprinted with amendments, Maidenhead: Commonwealth War Graves Commission, 1990.

ROGERS, C. 'War graves of the British Empire', *Sx.F.H.* **7**(2), 1986, 64-5. Lists 1st World War graves of Sussex men in various continental cemeteries.

C. *World War II*

ROBERTS, A.V.C. '1939-45 war dead of the Commonwealth and Empire', *Sx.F.H.* **11**(6), 1995, 227-8. List of Sussex men buried at Antwerp.

The War dead of the British Commonwealth and Empire: the register of the names of those who fell in the 1939-1945 war and are buried in cemeteries and churchyards in Surrey. 3 vols. Imperial War Graves Commission, 1959.

War dead of the British Commonwealth: the register of the names of those who fell in the 1939-1945 war and are buried in cemeteries and churchyards in Sussex. Commonwealth War Graves Commission, 1962.

D. *Local Rolls of Honour etc.*

Reference should be made to my *Surrey and Sussex parish registers, monumental inscriptions and wills,* vol. 2. of this series, for war memorials.

Cranleigh

WILKINS, PETER, & *Cranleigh's roll of honour 1914-1918, 1939-1945.* Cranleigh: Royal British Legion, Cranleigh & District Branch, 1997.

Danehill

'Men of our parish lost in the Great War 1914-18', *D.P.H.S.M.* **6**(5), 1999, 7-30. Biographical notes.

'Roll of honour: list of persons away on service 1939/45', *D.P.H.S.M.* **5**(4), 1995, 39-44. See also **5**(5), 1995, 32.

'Those away on service 1939-1945', *D.P.H.S.M.* **5**(4), 1995, 26-32. Biographical notes.

Guildford

Guildford and the Great War: roll of honour. Guildford: Surrey Advertiser, [192-?]

Merton

See Wimbledon

Wimbledon

Peace to the unconquered: a record of the honoured men of Wimbledon & Merton who fell in the Great War, 1914-1918, with notes of local activities during the same period. Mitchell Hughes and Clarke, 1921.

A record of the honoured men of Wimbledon & Merton who fell in the Great War, 1914-1918, with notes of local activities during the same period. Mitchell Hughes & Clarke, 1921.

E. *Regimental Histories, etc.*

1st Sussex Engineers

MEDHURST, LEN. '1st Sussex Engineers: prize distribution at Ripe', *F.R.* **5**(1), 1990, 6-7. Lists prize-winners, 1897.

2nd Queens Royal Regiment

DAVIS, JOHN. *The history of the Second Queen's Royal Regiment now the Queen's (Royal West Surrey) Regiment.* 7 vols. + folder of maps. Richard Bentley & Son, 1887-[1923]. Extensive: v.7 by H.C.Wylly.

2nd Royal Surrey

DAVIS, JOHN. *Historical records of the Second Royal Surrey, or Eleventh Regiment of Militia ...* Marcus Ward & Co., 1877. Includes 'appendix A: succession of officers of the Regiment from 1759 to 1876, with an index'.

5th Foot

WILLIAMS, J. ROBERT. 'Sussex veterans of the 5th Foot', *Sx.F.H.* **5**(5), 1983, 163-5. Includes list, 1813-27.

21st London

A war record of the 21st London Regiment (First Surrey Rifles) 1914-1919. [ ], 1927. Includes roll of honour and honours list.

Chertsey & Thorpe Volunteers

WEBB, CLIFF. 'Meeting of Chertsey and Thorpe volunteers', *R. & B.* **23**(4), 1997, 150-51. Includes list of subscribers, 1804.

Devonshire Regiment

ASLETT, WILLIAM C. 'Sussex men of the Devonshire Regiment who died in the Great War, 1914-1918', *Sx.F.H.* **13**(7), 1999, 233. List.

East Surrey Regiment

PAINE, J. 'A bibliography of the East Surrey Regiment', *Notes and queries* **160**, 1931, 59-60.

PAINE, J. 'The literature of a line regiment', *Journal of the Society for Army Historical Research* **13**(50), 1934, 107-13. The old 31st Regiment, later 1st Battalion, East Surrey Regiment. Bibliographical note.

ASTON, JOHN, & DUGGAN, L.M. *The history of the 12th (Bermondsey) Battalion East Surrey Regiment.* Union Press, 1936. During the Great War. Includes roll of honour, 1914-18.

CHRISTMAS, BRIAN W. 'Records of British officers taken prisoner in the European war, 1914-18', *E.Sy.F.H.S.J.* **12**(2), 1989, 17-19. Includes details of East Surrey Regiment prisoners.

DANIELL, DAVID SCOTT. *History of the East Surrey Regiment Volume IV. 1920-1952.* Ernest Benn, 1957. Continuation of Pearce's work; includes list of 'Honours and awards gained during 1939-1945 war'.

PEARCE, HUGH WODEHOUSE, & SLOMAN, HENRY STANHOPE. *History of the 31st Foot, Huntingdonshire Regiment, 70th Foot, Surrey Regt., subsequently 1st & 2nd Battalions of the East Surrey Regiment.* 3 vols. Spottiswoode, Ballantyne & Co., 1916-24. Extensive; v.3. includes 'nominal roll of warrant officers, non-commissioned officers, and men who were killed in action or died of wounds in the Great War, 1914-1919'.

Soldiers died in the Great War 1914-19. Part 36: the East Surrey Regiment. War Office, 1920. Reprinted Polstead: J.B.Hayward & Son, 1989.

LARKING, ALBERT. *History of the 4th V.B. East Surrey Regiment ...* [ ], 1912. Many names.

Lambeth & Southwark Volunteers

TAMPLIN, JOHN M.A. *The Lambeth and Southwark Volunteers, 1860-1960: a century of voluntary service in the Volunteers and Territorials, 1860-1960.* Trustees of the Regimental Historical Fund, 1965. Includes 'alphabetical roll', with brief biographies.

Mortlake Volunteers

ANDERSON, JOHN EUSTACE. *A short account of the Mortlake Company of the Royal Putney, Roehampton and Mortlake Volunteer Corps, 1803-6.* Richmond: R.W.Simpson, 1893. Brief pamphlet; some names.

O'SULLIVAN, MAUREEN. 'Mortlake volunteers', *E.Sy.F.H.S.J.* **11**(3), 1988, 38-9. List, c.1803.

North Pevensey Volunteers

WILLIAMS, J. ROBERT. 'North Pevensey Volunteers of the Napoleonic wars', *Sx.F.H.* **6**(2), 1984, 56-9; **6**(3), 1984, 95-8. Many names.

Queens

CLEAVER, ROSEMARY. 'The Queens Royal West Surrey Regiment: 8th Battalion reunion list', *R. & B.* **16**(1), 1989, 10-11. See also **16**(2), 1989, 58. Lists men who survived the First World War.

NEAVE, E.W.J. *History of the 11th Battalion, The Queens.* Brixton Free Press, 1931. Includes list of 'those who served, 1915-18'.

Soldiers died in the Great War 1914-19. Part 7. The Queen's Royal West Surrey Regiment). War Office, 1921. Reprinted Polstead: J.B.Hayward & Son, 1989.

BANNERMAN, RONALD. *4th the Queens Royal Regiment: an unofficial history, with chapters on the 2/5th Battalion.* Croydon: H.R. Grubb, 1931. Includes list of 'soldiers died', 1914-18, *etc.*

RILEY, J.P. *Soldiers of the Queen: the history of the Queen's Royal Surrey Regiment continuing into the Queen's Regiment 1959-1970.* Canterbury: Queen's Royal Surrey Regiment Association, [1988?]

Royal Sussex Regiment

PAINE, J. 'Books relating to the Royal Sussex Regiment', *Sussex county magazine* **21**, 1947, 148-51. Bibliographical note.

POWELL-EDWARDS, H.I. *The Sussex Yeomanry and 16th (Sussex Yeomanry) Battalion, Royal Sussex Regiment, 1914-1919.* Andrew Melrose, 1921. Includes rolls of officers and other ranks.

READMAN, A.E. *Records of the Royal Sussex Regiment: a catalogue.* West Sussex Record Office publication **57**. Chichester: West Sussex County Council, 1985.

RUTTER, OWEN. *The history of the Seventh (Service) Battalion the Royal Sussex Regiment 1914-1919.* Times Publishing, 1934.

TRIMEN, RICHARD. *An historical memoir of the 35th Royal Sussex Regiment of Foot.* Southampton: Southampton Times, 1873. Reprinted in facsimile, Lewes: East Sussex County Council, 1994. Includes list of 'Officers of the 35th (Royal Sussex) Regiment of Foot, from the 28th of June 1701 to the 31st of October 1871'.

HARWOOD, BRIAN. 'Royal Sussex Regiment: casualties in the Boer War', *Sx.G.L.H.* 3(2), 1981, 62. Brief list.

Rye Volunteers

VIDLER, LEOPOLD AMAN. *The story of the Rye Volunteers.* Rye: Rye Museum Commitee, 1954. Many names.

Surrey & Sussex Yeomanry

DAVIS, T.B. *The story of 98th Field Regiment (Surrey and Sussex Yeomanry Q.M.R.) R.A. (T.A.) and 144th Field Regiment (Surrey and Sussex Yeomanry) R.A. (T.A.) 1939-1946.* Hassocks: Ditchling Press, 1980. Includes roll of honour, and list of 'honours and awards'.

Surrey Territorials

JACKSON, ROBERT DONOVAN. *The territorials of Surrey, 1908-58.* Surbiton: Surrey Territorial & Auxiliary Forces Association, 1958. Brief.

Territorial battalions of the regiments of Surrey and their successors. Guildford: Queens Royal Surrey Regiment Museum, 1988. Detailed history of the various units.

Surrey Volunteers

CARDEW-RENDLE, H.C. 'Commissioned officers of the Surrey Volunteers, 1794-1845', *Notes and queries* **168**, 1935, 129-33, 146-50, 167-71, 184-7, 202-5, 220-24, 238-40, & 448. See also 230 & 283; **181**, 1941, 18-19; **194**, 1949, 543-4; **195**, 1950, 59-60, 81-2, 99-103, 126, 146-8, 170, & 210-14.

Surrey Yeomanry

HARRISON-AINSWORTH, E.D. *The history and war records of the Surrey Yeomanry (Queen Mary's Regt.) 1797-1928.* E.J.Larby, 1928. Includes various lists of officers and men.

Wimbledon Light Horse

O'SULLIVAN, MAUREEN. 'Wimbledon Light Horse (or Cavalry) Volunteers', *E.Sy.F.H.S.J.* 12(3), 1989, 34-6. List.

Swan masters

TICEHURST, N.F. 'Surrey swan-marks', *Sy.A.C.* **38**, 1929-30, 34-48. Lists marks and their owners.

Swordsmen

BISHOP, JOHN. 'William Peachey's swords', *Sx.F.H.* 5(4), 1982, 112-5. List of persons for whom Peachey made swords, 17th c.

Tallow Chandlers

LEPPARD, M.J. 'Tallow chandlers in East Grinstead', *Bulletin of the East Grinstead Society* **49**, 1991, 8-9. 18-19th c.

Teetotallers

HOLT, N. 'St. Leonards temperance pledge book', *Sx.F.H.* 6(6), 1985, 237-8. List of those who 'took the pledge' to abstain from alcohol, 1840-55.

Mitcham, Surrey. Berkley Teetotal Society, 1898: directory of members. 1 fiche in folder. East Surrey F.H.S. record publication, **51**. [199-].

Tennis Players

ANDERSON, IAN, *et al.* *History of the Pit Farm Tennis Club.* Guildford: the Club, 1997. Includes many names of players.

See also Cricketers

Tobacconists
See Wine Merchants

Tradesmen
In an age when small coin was in short supply, many tradesmen issued their own tokens. Studies of these provide the names of many tradesmen, and most of the works listed below are based on their evidence.

ANSCOMBE, BASIL. 'Sussex tokens', *Sussex county magazine* **7**, 1933, 121-9. List, 17-18th c.

CALDECOTT, J.B. 'Sussex 17th-century tokens', *British numismatic journal* **23**, 1940, 301-20. With names of issuers.

CALDECOTT, J.B. 'The Penfold bequest', *Sx.A.C.* **83**, 1943, 101-20. Includes names of Sussex token issuers, 17th c.

FIGG, WILLIAM. 'On Sussex tradesmen's tokens in the seventeenth century', *Sx.A.C.* **11**, 1859, 171-8; **18**, 1866, 163-4. See also **13**, 1861, 309.

HOOPER, WILFRID. 'Surrey seventeenth-century tokens', *Sy.A.C.* **48**, 1943, 17-30.

KING, ROY REDVERS. 'Seventeenth-century trade tokens of Sussex', *Sussex county magazine* **21**, 1947, 43-4. Brief note.

SMALLFIELD, J.S. 'Sussex tradesmen's tokens of the seventeenth century', *Sx.A.C.* **14**, 1872, 122-34.

WATERS, ARTHUR WILLIAM. *The token coinage of South London issued in the 18th and 19th centuries.* Leamington Spa: Simmons & Waters, 1904.

WILLIAMSON, GEORGE C. *Trade tokens issued in the seventeenth century in the county of Sussex, by corporations, merchants, tradesmen, etc.* Brighton: William J. Smith, [18--?]. Reprint of the Sussex portion of a larger work.

WILLIAMSON, GEORGE C. 'The trade tokens of Surrey issued in the seventeenth century', *Sy.A.C.* **10**, 1891, 79-95.

WETTON, J.L., & WETTON, N.L. 'The Surrey seventeenth-century traders' tokens', *Sy.A.C.* **56**, 1959, 29-50. See also **59**, 1962, 90-91. Includes list of issuers.

Bognor Regis
GOWLER, MICHAEL H. *Bognor's early trades and traders (1839-1871).* Bognor: Bognor Regis Local History Society, 1998.

Chichester
STEER, FRANCIS W. *Some Chichester tradesmen, 1652-1839.* Chichester papers **17**. Chichester: Chichester City Council, 1960. Includes various lists.

Croydon
MARTIN, EDWARD A. 'Token money in Croydon', *Transactions of the Croydon Natural History and Scientific Society* **8**, 1915-18, 1-4. Identifies token issuers.

Danehill
LUCAS, PHIL. 'Trades and occupations 1840-1900', *D.P.H.S.M.* **1**(10), 1981, 15-26. Lists tradesmen, 19-20th c.

Farnham
MERSON, R.A. 'A preliminary note on the Farnham seventeenth-century traders tokens', *F.M.S.Q.N.* **3**(10), 1974, 18-19.

PARKS, PEGGY. 'Some Farnham shopkeepers in 1887', *F.M.S.Q.N.* **9**(1), 1990, 19-21; **9**(2), 1990, 42-5. List.

Godstone
SAALER, MARY. 'Godstone traders in the 1850's', *L.H.R.* **26**, 1987, 35-7. Brief article

Westbourne
ELLACOTT, PETER. *Trades people of Westbourne, 1845-1938.* Bygone Westbourne 1. Westbourne: Westbourne Local History Group, 1981. Includes lists of tradesmen from directories.

Visitors
FARRANT, SUE. 'Who visited Brighton in 1769?', *Sx.G.L.H.* **3**(1), 1981, 16-18. List of visitors from the *Sussex weekly advertiser.*

Watermen & Lightermen
COTTRELL, ROBERT J. *Surname index to the Company of Watermen & Lightermen, London.* Fiche in 9 folders. Bexleyheath: R.J.Cottrell, [1991]-6. Apprenticeship bindings, *etc.,* 1692-1949. Includes many names from the south bank of the Thames.

Whitsters

MONTAGUE, E.N. *A study of the textile bleaching and printing industry in Mitcham and Merton from 1590 until 1870.* Merton Historical Society, 1992. Many names of whitsters, bleachers and calico printers.

Wine Merchants

'Sussex wine-merchants and tobacconists, 1633 to 1635', *Sx.A.C.* **36**, 1888, 247-8. Brief list.

Witches

EWEN, L'ESTRANGE, ed. *Witch hunting and witch trials: the indictments for witchcraft from records of 1373 assizes held for the Home Circuit, 1559-1736.* Kegan Paul, Trench, Trubner Co., 1929. Evidence from Essex, Kent, Surrey, Sussex and Hertfordshire.

Wood Carvers

'Newdigate, Surrey: records of wood carving in church of St. Peter', *Sy.A.C.* **66**, 1969, 128-30. Includes names of wood-carvers.

Wood Colliers

See Charcoalburners

Wool Merchants

PELHAM, R.A. 'The distribution of wool merchants in Sussex in 1296', *Sx.N.Q.* **4**, 1933, 161-3. List from subsidy rolls.

PELHAM, R.A. 'The distribution of wool merchants in Sussex (c.1330)', *Sx.N.Q.* **4**, 1933, 67-9. Includes list from the subsidy roll.

See also Ship Owners & Masters

Author Index

40

Family Name Index

Place Name Index